T0209311

Well, Actually ....
Thank you, Momma

Holly Marie and Carla Cross

WESTBOW
PRESS®
A DIVISION OF THOMAS NELSON
& ZONDERVAN

This book is a work of non-fiction. Unless otherwise noted, the author and the publisher make no explicit guarantees as to the accuracy of the information contained in this book and in some cases, names of people and places have been altered to protect their privacy.

WestBow Press books may be ordered through booksellers or by contacting:

WestBow Press
A Division of Thomas Nelson & Zondervan
1663 Liberty Drive
Bloomington, IN 47403
www.westbowpress.com
844-714-3454

ISBN: 979-8-3850-0385-3 (sc)
ISBN: 979-8-3850-0386-0 (hc)
ISBN: 979-8-3850-0387-7 (e)

Library of Congress Control Number: 2023913724

Print information available on the last page.

WestBow Press rev. date: 9/26/2023

Prologue

September 4, 2021, 8:23 p.m. …time of death. This was the end of Britney's life, the end of her time spent on earth but not the end of her story.

Brit, as we all do, had a dash between the day of her birth and the day of her death. During her twenty year dash, she lived a life that impacted multitudes, leaving not just memories but a remarkable legacy. Brit's legacy will not be forgotten by any of us who got to witness her living it, but to keep that legacy alive for those who come after us, I have to tell her story.

This is Britney's remarkable story! I'm the only one who can recount it in full because I'm the only one who lived it with her every second of every single day. To fully understand her story, you have to know me and the religious lifestyle that made me who I am. This culture was the basis of every decision I made and ultimately the reason I second guessed myself with every decision I made regarding her care.

So, before I tell Britney's story, you need to know mine, her father's and some of the distinctions of the culture we were born into. It was a religious culture that we would ultimately raise our children in, until they reached their mid teens.

Britney's father and I were both born and raised in a religion that far exceeded your typical Sunday meetings, occasional Bible studies and annual revivals. A religion-or, as we called it "our Christian family", took precedence over our physical family and any other relationships we may have desired to have outside of the church. We had no real communication or interaction with the outside world. Therefore, all of our friendships, and most definitely courtships, were developed within the church. Relationships between husbands and wives, along with raising children, were closely monitored and expected to be done in a way that they felt was the godly way they, being a few select men better known as the leaders, who manipulated God's Word to support their man-made doctrine and usurp control over all those they felt were unworthy of leadership. The one known and adhered-to fundamental was that men were the head of their wives, and married or not, women had no voice. We were expected, if married, to be keepers of the home, pleasers of our husbands and to bear and raise children "in the nurture and admonition of the Lord." We were required to submit ourselves to our husbands. Our body was his body. It was preached, "Husbands, love your wives as Christ so loved the church," and they were admonished to protect us from the world and lead us into the way of everlasting.

There were husbands in that church who truly did love their wives "as Christ so loved the church." They did honor them, respect them and cherish them but the majority of the husbands, through complete naivety, used their authority over their wives to decide everything involving the family unit. There was not the equal but separate mindset. Instead, the man being the head of the family, meant he was responsible for making all the decisions with little or no input from his wife.

The truth is, although that sounded godly and irreproachable, it was just a deceiving way of controlling every aspect of every life in the church. As for those women who weren't married, not only were they looked at with pity; they were admonished to serve the church and help young wives and mothers to take up slack in the church kitchen and find their glory and worth in joyfully serving others. The true meaning of that was, to carry out the menial tasks that the men felt "the weaker vessel" was capable of carrying out.

Most of us, by God's grace, have left this religion or, as I like to call it, the culture we were raised in. Because truthfully, it was just another man-made religion but one so controlling and rule oriented that it was a culture and not just a religion. For every surmised mistake, there was a punishment and it was often in front of the church members, directly from the pulpit. Any personal thought, conviction or opinion voiced by a woman was completely discounted as someone not being properly led by her father, husband or any other leader of the church. This thought process carried over into every marriage because we were only allowed to marry within the church. There was no dating. We were never alone without a chaperone and had no real conversation about what either of us desired in our marriage or future family unit. We built our courtships and marriages on serving the church which ultimately meant following the rules. For us women, that meant performing and toeing the line so there was no shame brought on our husbands or fathers.

While this may sound arcane, when it's all you've ever known and really all you've ever witnessed, it is your normal. We are all born into this world a clean slate and we become what we experience. So even though I often questioned how any of this could be right, I had nothing to compare it with. I had no standard except the one I had grown up in and the people I had been influenced by, some of whom I even had great respect for, desiring their approval.

Most of us had no real contact with the outside world besides trips to the grocery store, doctor's visits and so on. Most children were homeschooled, though some did attend public school. Typically boys, but rarely girls, went to school and this is where I have to give my dad credit. I did go to public school and was raised, by the church's standards, very independently. He took a lot of flak for that, but in the end, it certainly paid off. Had I been raised as the majority of the girls were, I could not have become the advocate I was for Britney. I wasn't afraid to go with my gut and do what I knew she needed and I certainly didn't need a man to tell me how to do it. That ended up being a blessing, much in my favor, as I took on the role of caring and advocating for Brit on my own. I was rarely agreed with or supported and I spent much of my time fighting against those who should have had her best interests at heart. I fought to get her the care and treatment she needed and I learned to do it solely on my own. I learned early on to not depend on, or even discuss it with, anyone besides her care team.

I could go on and on, but this book isn't about me; it's about Britney. My mother, her mother and all of the women in Brit's family were living this life of obedience, naivety, lack of grace, withholding of mercy and overall oppression. *Oppression being* the word used by one of the leaders who left the church and is willing to humble himself and speak the truth.

So, all this said, when I found out I was having a girl, and long before I heard the words Asperger's syndrome or chronic disease, I was fully committed to raising her to love God and seek His will in her life but to do it with integrity. I wanted her to know her ability and be confident in her worth, showing grace, mercy and humility but never with her head hung in shame. I didn't want her doubting her capability of rising as high as she wanted to reach and I didn't want her feeling she was less than. I didn't want her identifying as the "weaker vessel" as it was used in the context I had heard all of my life. Most of all, as with both of my children, I wanted her to know that she was loved, cherished, supported, rooted for and believed in and that my arms and lap were open for her no matter how old she was or what the circumstances were. I wanted her to believe, and I do believe she had this confidence, that I would stay beside her. That I would fight battles I could never have dreamed up, much less comprehend, and that I would never give up on her. I would follow her lead, support her decisions and do whatever I could possibly do to help her succeed. Although I couldn't have imagined what was in store for either of us when I heard "It's a girl", I do believe that on September 4, 2021, at 8:23 p.m., Britney knew I was there for her. She knew I still supported her decision and I was there to help her through until the very end.

This is her story, written in short, by Britney in the form of her college essay.

> I was diagnosed with Asperger Syndrome at the age of three. At the time, not much was commonly known about Asperger's, so my parents took me to several doctors for advice on how to manage it. The doctors all told them the same thing: Not to try and teach me or make me do anything because, according to them, I would never be capable of learning, communicating, or understanding anything. But my parents knew that that wasn't true, at least to a degree, and helped me prove the doctors wrong. Without the support and determination of my parents, I would not be who I am today.

First off, I am very lucky to be really, really low on the Autism Spectrum, and I haven't had near as much trouble with it as the people who are higher on the Spectrum. Each person on the Spectrum is different, and has different capabilities. My parents knew that the doctors were wrong about me because I was already learning and talking normally for my age. The main challenge was that it overstimulated me to be around people and to socialize with them, and when my parents made me, I threw fits. But instead of allowing me to isolate myself and ignoring the fits, my parents pushed me out of my comfort zone and disciplined me when I needed it. They never made excuses or allowances for me because I had Asperger's, and though they received some flak for it, they never compromised to make things easier on themselves.

When I was still three, my mother enrolled me in a sort of pre-school for kids who need speech therapy to help prepare me for elementary school. I hated it, saying that the kids were smelly and too loud (which they were!). But my mom knew I had to learn how to play with and behave around kids my own age. My mom had to drag me up the stairs and into the building every school day for two years. Then into Cooke Kindergarten for a year, and then into Gerard Elementary for about three. Yep, when I said my mother had determination I wasn't kidding. Around the end of third grade I began to be more comfortable at school, and started enjoying it. It had taken nearly six years of me screaming and being dragged into school, but I finally walked into the school and into class on my own.

Those doctors would never have guessed I'd be capable of doing the things I've done. They said I wouldn't learn, but I'm in my school's top ten percent and am applying to colleges. They said I wouldn't understand or communicate with people, but now I'm very involved in my high school's FFA Chapter, I ran for and secured the position of Chapter Secretary two years in a row, and I compete in both Leadership and Career Development Events; all of which involve communication and people skills, plus a fair amount of learning too!

But I never would have had a chance at becoming who I am today and proving the doctors wrong had I not been raised me the way I was. They were determined to give me the best chance at a happy and successful life that they could, even when some questioned their actions. Because of them, I am able to be comfortable around people and I even enjoy going to school, which I used to hate! And because I go to school I have been able to be a part of the Cleburne FFA Chapter, which has given me confidence and helped me develop my people skills further. None of that would have been possible without my parents' sheer grit, and I will never be able to fully express how grateful to them I am for the life they have given me. All I can do is show them how far I can go with the opportunities I am given.

Chapter 1

I didn't like being born! Most people don't remember it, but I do...and I hated it! Everything was bright and loud and I know I remember it because I didn't see that doctor again until I was four, and I recognized her. Some people don't believe me, but if I tell the ones that were there about it, they look at me weird and I know they know I'm for real!

—Britney

April 15, 2001, 5:33 a.m. After fifteen hours of labor, Britney let us all know she had arrived. She continued to let us all know for the next eleven hours straight. She screamed so loudly that the nurse, trying to give me a break, took her to the nursery...then quickly brought her back! I paced the floor, I swaddled, I checked her diaper and I did all the things moms do to comfort their babies. Britney was not my first. She came three years after her brother, an extremely docile and easy baby. I babysat in my preteen years, up until I got married. I even made money teaching moms to sleep train, or get their babies on schedules, and I could sooth the most difficult case of colic out there. Still, nothing worked on Britney and nothing made her madder than me trying to breastfeed her. My baby girl looked like, as Britney later described herself, a mad ET. At four pounds, twelve ounces, eighteen inches and full of fight, she was a sight to behold.

Now, breastfeeding was my natural talent. We knew she was getting enough milk, but just to make sure, we decided to try a bottle. She was still mad and I was concerned because she was a preemie and didn't weigh a full five pounds. It was evident that, even at a few days, she was a mad little girl-not hurting, not scared or sleepy …just mad.

Then, I figured it out! She would drink a bottle if she was propped on a pillow, not being held or touched. For the next feeding, I sat with my legs crossed, placed a pillow on my lap, laid her on it and nursed her without holding her up against me. She nursed a lot…a whole lot, and she continued to for the next five months as long as she laid on a pillow, not touching me. She gained a pound a week for the first ten weeks and turned into a chunk. But, she still didn't tolerate touching. She didn't like people around her. She didn't like much of anything actually, but would be happy for hours if left alone. She was happy lying in her crib, staring at the ceiling fan. As she got old enough to move herself around, she'd stretch long ways on my lap and tilt her head up to eat but kick my knees the entire time.

But, back to her birth and the early days following. After all the screaming subsided, I was able to revel in how beautiful my baby girl was. She had a head full of black, curly hair and this perfect tiny mouth. She had the darkest eyes that seemed to take in everything at once. Despite her perfection, I had a nagging feeling that something was wrong.

At one week, she started rolling just as her brother had. Only, her brother rolled to get a better view of people. Britney rolled to get to the wall, or especially the brick hearth, to scratch at it. She was never interested in bright baby toys or even Zach's toys. She wanted to touch the texture on the wall or bricks. This behavior wasn't the only oddity when compared to Zach or other babies I had cared for. She would lie on the floor for hours, staring at the ceiling fan, sometimes so intently that she would hold her breath. She was happiest if left alone in her crib the ceiling fan spinning for her to look at and a floor fan on high to block out all noise. Life would have been much more peaceful had I left her alone.

But,even then, I knew something wasn't right and I needed to push her out of her comfort zone. I couldn't let her preferences dictate our family life but had I, our lives would have been a lot more peaceful. Even at a very early age, she would scream for hours when she didn't get her way but I was equally determined and that made for some long hard days. Eventually, I learned to better work with her and we both grew to compromise. Learning to put myself in what I imagined to be her shoes, was a turning point in my ability to not only understand her, but to weigh each situation and deal with it accordingly.

With me showing a little more compassion and understanding, instead of relying solely on discipline, Britney's screaming calmed down. I was learning what set her off. It seemed that we were settling into a routine at five months but then…she decided to talk. Literally talk. Not the "I'm sure she said Momma" type of speech; she was much more direct. I wasn't overly surprised because Zach was saying *hi* and *bye* and the typical *momma* and *daddy* pretty early too. Only Britney didn't say those words; she said, "No" and she very clearly meant *no*!

Our social circle had pretty much ceased to exist, because she screamed every time we were around people. But, as I learned to work with her, that started to change. We were getting out and around others more and now there was an element of surprise. When we were out on play dates, the older children would eat their lunch and the babies would breastfeed or bottle feed…except Britney. When she saw the other kids eating solid food, she took one look at the bottle and yelled *no*! She wanted solid food and anyone within yelling distance, without a doubt, knew what she wanted. She didn't just use her new word to get what she wanted, she could turn the word *no* into a fully opinionated statement. When I dared a trip to the grocery store, and she wasn't screaming herself into oblivion, every little lady that leaned over her infant seat to comment on my beautiful little baby was greeted with a very loud *no*!

About the time we reached six months, that nagging feeling that had started at the hospital became a valid concern. There were too many things that were just not right. Too many things set her off and these weren't just fits, teething or normal kid things. But still, I ignored it and we went on.

By the time Britney was one year old, she had developed an even more rigid system of order. A week's worth of clothes had to be laid out every Sunday. The red spoon could only be used with the white bowl and a calendar was hung in her room that she constantly checked as she went about her day. Even though our social life was far from normal, we still attended church. For us, that meant Zach and their father sitting in the service while Britney and I sat in the car. We couldn't even change our seating in the car without a massive meltdown or change any routine without a huge upset that went on for hours. It wasn't for lack of discipline, and yes, I'm going to use that word.

Britney was disciplined, as you read in the essay she wrote while applying for colleges. She attributes much of her success to being held to a standard and disciplined with the understanding that every child is different and not all children respond to the same methods. She was held to that standard with me acknowledging that not all of her outbursts were normal childhood behavior. I had begun trying to help her with sensory issues long before I ever heard the words *Autism* or *Asperger's syndrome* and we were making some progress but, to top that off, she started having some weird physical issues. Before long, they became far more concerning than her social ones.

Britney was spiking reoccurring fevers and was obviously in horrible pain when they peaked. She wasn't able to tell us exactly where the pain was because, once again, Asperger's syndrome made communication hard for her. We did have our suspicions about where the pain was the strongest because when it hit, she wouldn't move her hips or legs. These episodes resulted in numerous trips to the ER, many x-rays along with other scans and multiple blood draws. Somewhere along the line, one of her specialists decided to send off her blood for genetic testing. Back then, we had to send her blood to Germany and we had to wait six to nine months for the results. That's a long time to wait when your child's symptoms are getting worse and her episodes are getting closer together. We had no choice. So we settled in for the wait and managed her symptoms the best we could.

During the wait for the genetic testing to come back, labs were drawn here at home and it was confirmed that Britney had Juvenile Rheumatoid Arthritis. Some type of fever syndrome was suspected but we wouldn't have a diagnosis until the testing was complete. Still, her symptoms were getting worse and I wasn't sure it all went together so I started searching and reading all that I could find. There was no Google back then, and there wasn't a lot to go on unless you knew exactly what you were looking for, and I didn't. I was at loose ends.

One thing that worked in our favor was that Britney's granddad, "Doc", owned his own practice. When one of his previous mentors decided to retire from the medical school, he came to work for Doc. I had known Dr. B for years and he took an interest in Brit right away. He saw me struggling to find answers and he was often the patient recipient of my extensive questions and harebrained ideas. He quietly supported me and I rarely walked into my dad's clinic without Dr. B suggesting I look into some sort of testing or handing me some printed out information he'd found. I thought highly of him, and trusted his years of experience, so when he suggested that he ask some medical students to do some research, I gladly took him up on it. What they found ended up being my biggest source of information at the time. Not only was it informative and helpful, but it eased my mind. Reading through it made me realize, even more, that it wasn't going to be an easy road but at least I had something to work with. Ultimately Dr. B, working with Brit's pediatrician, came up with a treatment regimen that would control and drastically decrease her reoccurring ear infections. That was a huge hurdle that we overcame and I'll always be extremely grateful for the time and effort that Dr. B invested in Brit and I.

In her early crawling days, Britney would empty bottom drawers, climb in and close herself in. While I was cooking, she'd close herself up in the empty plasticware drawer, where she was perfectly happy in the dark with her blankie. For the most part, she was happy on her own and didn't interact much with any of us. Other times, she would search out her brother, Zach, and whack him with his plastic golf club. Those were the times that my little angel showed her little devil side. She could go from one to the other in a split second with very little provocation or warning.

Although challenging at times, I loved Britney's independence. I had never had much use for prissy girls and surely didn't want to raise one. Early on, I had decided she would not be allowed to dissolve into tears because her hair wasn't right or someone looked at her wrong, and

I was hoping for no excessive squealing. It soon became evident she was not going to be a squealer and she didn't have a prissy bone in her body. She was much like her mother; stubborn, opinionated and independent. I could raise this girl and I was excited to do it.

I knew my little girl was beyond smart and you couldn't get anything past her but when it came to social skills, she was woefully behind her peers. She barely tolerated other kids and had no interest in human interaction. She rarely looked at us or acknowledged anyone's presence. When we spent time with kids from our church, she'd stay in her stroller, preferably covered by a blanket.

By the time Britney was two, she had thirty-three stuffed animals that had to be lined up perfectly every night in some order that only she understood. Occasionally, I'd move an animal just to introduce flexibility into her rigid structure. She would scream for hours, because the disruption of her order was unbearable to her, and I often wondered how she would cope with the chaos life would throw at her. We live in an unpredictable world; a world that doesn't embrace rigid routines or seemingly odd behaviors.

Even with these things going on, at times she'd act like a typical toddler and I'd hope things were going to even out. Sometimes she would tolerate other children, especially the older ones, and she was a quick learner who could compensate by modeling the play of others. Britney's example of typical behavior came from her friend Courtney. Even as a toddler, Courtney, was confident and she could take charge. If Britney could mimic Courtney, she could navigate social situations.

Britney was two years old when my suspicions turned to concern and I started to seriously admit to myself that there could be a known name to the reason she was so different from other children. These differences were becoming less subtle and more blatant. She had the vocabulary of a ten year old. She was picking out science books at the library and had no real interest in children's books. She had no use for anything age appropriate for a toddler. She was more interested in facts, especially obscure facts, and we were amazed at what she knew but had no idea where her knowledge came from.

By the time she was two and a half, I knew it was time to consult a doctor, so I turned to the one who knew Britney best ...my dad. I told him I knew Britney was different but I didn't know what was wrong. He was hesitant at first. Being my dad, and Britney's granddad, made it difficult for him but I had to know and understand what I was dealing with so I could learn to help her. He finally admitted that he had his suspicions and said he felt like she had a form of autism along with obsessive compulsive disorder (OCD)

I didn't have a clue if my dad was right but by now she was heading toward being three years old and past the ideal age for early-childhood intervention. I had no idea which direction to go or who to ask for help. I remember being alone in my bedroom, staring into the darkness while the kids were in bed. All I could think of was the movie *Rain Man* and I felt sick. I wasn't sure I agreed with my dad, but now at least I had some direction and I had a word to research. Minutes later I was online reading about others with the same symptoms. I cried that night. I cried because what I was reading about wasn't what I wanted for my daughter. I cried because I didn't want her to struggle or be different. I wanted her to be happy. I wanted her to have relationships and to know what love was and not just the idea of love; I wanted her to feel it. One thing I did know was, I would not attach a label to my child if I wasn't 100 percent sure.

The scorn from some in my biological family, and church family, for me thinking about labeling Brit was awful. Their opinions were really irrelevant because Britney's future was at stake. I had to be certain for my sake, but most importantly for Britney's, that she actually had autism. I thought that if she did, this would be a battle we would fight for a while. We would win and life would go on. It was that simple.

Chapter 2

I remember hurting and being in pain but I just thought it went along with everything else that was going on with me. I thought that the pain was just something added to not liking smells, noises, crowds or people in general. I didn't know that the pain was separate from all of my sensory issues.

—Britney

We had been seeing her pediatrician, Dr. Bryan, practically on a weekly basis. We had a great relationship with him and he knew Britney very well. I called his office, asked for a consult and drove Brit to see him. That was the second time I heard the words *autism* and the first time I heard the definition of Asperger's syndrome. He was hesitant to tell me but he knew me well enough to know that I knew something was wrong. He figured that I wouldn't fall apart if he told me what he suspected before sending us to another specialist. Little did I know, that me not falling apart, set the tone of our relationship over many really big hurdles and some pretty scary conversations during the next twenty years. That conversation led to extensive testing and many doctor and diagnostician appointments. Some of these could have been avoided had I not been so reluctant to put a label on my daughter. After the seventh doctor diagnosed Asperger's syndrome, I gave in and started trying to figure out how to fix it, because that's what I do. I fix things and I was sure this could be fixed, wrapped up and put behind us by kindergarten. That was my goal and I had every intention of seeing it through only, I didn't have a clue where to begin until a friend advised me to call our public school system and ask about early childhood intervention.

This is where my upbringing in our church became a big issue. Even though I was raised in the culture of this church, my saving grace was that I went to public schools and had developed relationships in that environment. I was exposed to the existence of strong women who could think for themselves. It became a big problem when my church family, and even some in my biological family, deliberately started gossiping and throwing out opinions making me, along with others, doubt myself. It's easy to question yourself and hard to trust your God given instincts but even more so, when you're a woman raised in that culture. When you're trusting 'worldly' people and their influences on your children, how do you keep from becoming 'of the world' yourself?

Still, I was determined to have Britney fixed, cured, normal or whatever you want to call it by kindergarten, so I made that call to the school. The first meeting was just with a diagnostician. I didn't tell my husband because I knew it wasn't going to sit well with him. I was told that they would test her and, if indeed she was on the autism spectrum, they would do all they could to mainstream her in to the school setting. We could work through this with them, and do our part at home, or we could just let her be but her behavior would only get worse with no intervention. After meeting with the school, I took her to an appointment at a well known place in Fort Worth. They told me that she probably wouldn't learn to do much but we could help control the raging with meds. To me, that wasn't even an option and we never went back.

All in all, from age one to age three, Britney was diagnosed with Hans Asperger's syndrome, dysmotility that caused megacolon, frequent kidney and bladder infections, juvenile rheumatoid arthritis and constant ear infections.

As I began to seek help our life became schedules, calendars, special diets and supplements. Life changed in other ways too. We stopped saving for college and began to invest in the best interventions available. We learned to plan ahead and to never do anything spur of the moment.

We learned to adapt. More than that, I stepped out of my comfort zone, began to live my life in the open and learned to live with the critics. There wasn't a lot of choice when it came to being noticed. If we walked into a grocery store, everyone knew we had arrived and I mean everyone. Britney would quickly get overstimulated, the screaming would begin and it was deafening. Life at home was hectic too. If a pea rolled to the far side of the plate, Britney's day was ruined. She would get upset and begin to rock back and forth, banging her head, inconsolably. Zach went on with life like nothing was happening. The tensions between the kid's father and me just kept rising.

I placed my bet on our school system and went to my first ARD meeting on September 22, 2003. It was scary for a girl, who had only graduated from high school, to go into a meeting with six professional women. These 'worldly' women were all in proper attire. They had makeup on and their hair in the latest styles while I sat there with no makeup, long uncut hair and with clothes deemed modest by church standards. But, the reality was, that I was beyond modest and into the realm of dowdy and I felt it. Still, I was willing to do whatever it took to give my daughter the best chance possible and that made any insecurity I felt, fall to the wayside. Plus, this was just a small battle compared to what I knew was coming.

I knew that when I presented the thought of our soon-to-be three year old starting school to my husband, being as he was a man raised with the principles of the church, a storm would start brewing …and it did! No fighting, just silent anger because he still didn't agree with the diagnosis. There wasn't dissension just at home, but at the church. That was a problem because they tended to have the final word in all things. Not only was I accused of doing my children wrong by sending my three year old *female* to a worldly school, but I was accused of coddling Britney unnecessarily . The church and family tongues were wagging and the long and short of it was, that I wasn't able to adequately care for my child by their standards. There were small stretches where I let their opinions cast doubt, but when I truly focused on Britney, their thoughts and opinions faded into the background. Still, there were times that my insecurities got the best of me.

The gossiping, coupled with my insecurities, made the wait from

September to April seem to drag on and on. Before starting school, there was a lot of testing be done to make sure she qualified for the school's services. Plus, she had to be three years old to start, so it was a busy five months, and I should have spent more time living in the moment, and not in my head. But as stubborn and determined as I was to get her help, I really doubted and wrestled with my decision. What kind of mom, especially one who has the opportunity to stay home, sends her three-year-old to school? What kind of mom sends her toddler with a new diagnosis of autism, plus pending physical diagnoses, off to a place where *worldly* strangers are going to spend hours with them each week doing what I was supposed to be doing at home?

I did! I sent my three-year-old little girl with *special needs*, something that was taboo to say out loud, along with multiple physical problems, to school. There was a time I was ashamed to admit that but not now. The decision to stand up for my daughter, and do what was right for her, caused me to lose a lot of sleep and a lot of friends and it ostracized me from much of my church and biological family. It caused a lot more stress between Brit's father and me but I'm not ashamed of that decision and haven't been for a very long time.

A recommended child psychologist suggested that we pad her room and put her in there when she was raging and her father leaned toward that thinking also. He wanted to let her be, and that would have been much easier, but I knew that Britney was brilliant and had such potential. I wasn't willing to let her mind go to waste just because I didn't want to put the time and effort into training her. In training her, I didn't want to force her into any preconceived mold but wanted to give her the tools she needed to reach the incredible potential that I saw in her. I knew it was going to be hard, and I knew Britney wasn't going to cut me any slack, but I was the one person more stubborn than she was and I was not going to give up on her.

It was a dark time. I thought Asperger's syndrome was our big battle. I felt like it was trying to define us and I wasn't going to let it. I was determined to win, to help Britney win. I thought AS would be the biggest battle I would ever help Britney fight. I couldn't possibly have been more wrong!

As far as going with our public school system instead of the highly acclaimed center that was suggested, that was one of the best and most blessed decisions I've ever made in my life. That decision shaped Britney into who she became and gave her the tools she needed to move ahead. They taught me more than I could have ever learned from any institution and, most importantly, the ones who cared for Brit in the school became her family, our family. Britney, Zach, and I gained so much support. As Britney moved through school, our family of teachers, support staff and community, grew bigger and bigger. The bonds grew stronger and they were all there with her, some in person and so many in spirit, when she took her last breath.

When I had to be at the hospital with Brit, it was important to me that Zachary was getting some much-needed support. It was a load off my mind to know that he was being taken care of by family members. He had those who loved him as their own and, it was an added bonus that he had cousins his age to play with. All along, Zach was the big brother for Britney. None of this was fair to him, but he was resilient. He never lost his sense of humor, never showed anger or acted out and he relished any time I could focus on him but, never demanded extra attention. He adapted much faster than I did. He knew how to take care of his sister and knew what she needed. He never missed a beat when it came to moving between his world and hers. As Brit became less social, Zach continued to create a network of friends and participated in activities that brought a sense of normalcy to our lives. He paved the way in many aspects, one of them being school.

Because of Zachary's example, when at three years old, Brit got enrolled into the preschool for kids with special needs, she had an idea of what school was all about. She had her struggles, but she began to get the help she needed, and I learned as much as I possibly could. My goal was to help her become a typical child by the time she started kindergarten. I wanted her to be able to cope with life and not be overcome by the sounds, smells, sights and general disorder that is part of the human experience. I would watch young girls walk by, talking and laughing about some topic that was only funny in the land of young girls, and I wanted that for my daughter. I knew I could get her there. I was determined to fight and give Brit as normal of a childhood as possible. I knew I could teach her how to navigate and function in our world.

A large part of our world revolved around our church, and church was not a place she enjoyed at all. She didn't like the crowds, the noise of the singing drove her over the edge and the preaching well, she had no use for that at all. The truth is I didn't either, but I still knew that I needed to teach her to navigate this world we lived in and our life in the church seemed to be the best place, outside of our home, to start.

Sitting through a church service was one of Brit's biggest challenges and she made sure everyone knew how much she hated it. But, even with her disruptions, she was obviously taking in some of what she was hearing. One Sunday, after a particular sermon on the sins of idolatry, Brit marched straight up to the stage and, with her feet firmly planted and her hands on her hips, she informed the preacher that she saw nothing wrong with Dollar Tree and enjoyed shopping there. Not only did she say she liked to go there; she also made it very clear that she intended to keep on going there.

Chapter 3

My Mom dragged me through the gate at preschool. I was mad and I didn't like the kids: they smelled and they weren't smart enough to be four years old. I was a high functioning child! I liked to talk about the stars and the planets and I liked to think about how old dinosaurs were. I would say I hated people, but it wasn't the people...it was what they made me do. Why should I go to school, and why were the others kids crazy? They sounded like they were yelling and it was uncomfortable. Sometimes my teacher would lay on me to keep me from running away. I wasn't trying to leave, I was just trying to be alone. I'm not sure where I would have gone or what would have happened if she hadn't stopped me.

—Britney

Our family was getting a lot of advice from people with good intentions, some not so much. They made insensitive statements like "Maybe she's shy", "Maybe she just doesn't like crowds" or "Maybe she's naughty". Even her father and I disagreed. Do we let her be herself or should we try to fix this? He understood Britney had issues but said to just let her be. He was reluctant to proceed with early intervention and felt like our family was fine, that we could adjust. The word *autism* became a bone of contention in our home. The same diagnostician who had once told me, "Some parents with children like this have an empty room to put them in when they are enraged," also told me "Don't try to fix her; you can't fix her." I was going to fix her no matter what it took. She deserved so much more than to be labeled without some effort put forth to help her succeed.

My biggest resource in helping Britney became our school system. I turned to them for help because they spent hours with Britney and they understood her issues. Her teachers became my lifeline. Preschool classes were only twice a week and on the days between, I remained focused on her social skills. During this new phase of life, Britney began to get even more odd cold and flu-like symptoms but she still managed to attend school. I was thinking the fevers and joint pain were both by-products of her exposure to other kids and typical childhood germs. Was this a typical first year of school with a child who was anything but typical? I was in uncharted territory and I genuinely didn't know.

Among Britney's reoccurring symptoms, were the more frequent fevers. Her temperature would be normal, then spike to 105°-106° in a matter of minutes. Cold baths, ibuprofen and ice packs were routine in our home. Britney would scream and repeat, " It hurts," over and over, but she couldn't tell us where she felt pain. She didn't want to walk. I assumed it was because she didn't want her feet touching the floor. I thought the body aches were caused by the fever and magnified by her sensory issues.

At this time, she was still under the misdiagnosis of TRAP syndrome (tumor necrosis factor receptor associated periodic syndrome). It wouldn't be until years later that we would find out it was a misdiagnosis.

About the same time Britney's fevers were spiking, she began having urinary problems. She had multiple urinary tract infections, which were highly unusual for a four-year-old child. Again, I blamed Asperger's syndrome. Control is a big issue with AS kids and holding their urine is not uncommon. We tried to encourage her to empty her bladder regularly. We had a clock in the living room with stickers at twelve, two, four, six, eight, and ten. It was a visual reminder for her to go to the bathroom because for Britney to function, she needed everything to be visual.

AS kids often have trouble processing specific types of information. Brit loved the solar system and could explain huge concepts like how the universe was formed but, feelings sent her brain into overload. Even common phrases like "Hi, Momma" were difficult for her to express. She could ask for me but couldn't look me in the face and say, "Momma". It was too personal and totally out of her comfort zone.

I remember when Zach was born, telling myself that my kids would grow up hearing me say "I love you" as often as it could possibly be said. Where Zach responded to these words appropriately, Brit didn't respond at all. I didn't take it personally because I knew that she just couldn't express those feelings. But one day when I said, "I love you, Brit", she responded with "Well, I want to love you, but I'm not sure I do. Still, I do like you better than anyone else." That was Britney's way. She was always brutally honest and to the point. Despite the typical perception that we have in thinking kids on the spectrum have no empathy, she did. Though she couldn't show it, she would always find ways to let you know.

In July 2006, Britney's fever once again spiked to 104°. As many times before, she was lying on the bed with her legs in a sitting position and she wouldn't let us straighten her hips. She screamed and sobbed when the pediatrician tried to examine her. He sent us right to the emergency room. Even there, they couldn't straighten her legs and transported her in a wagon supported by pillows. X-rays and blood work revealed inflammation that, once again, confirmed rheumatoid arthritis. The results explained Britney's pain and possible cause. It also explained what she couldn't express; the pain was coming from the inflamed joints in her hips and legs. Though this was not our first trip to the ER, this was the trip that started what became our new life. A life of multiple emergency trips, countless admissions and weeks on end in a pediatric hospital where we had more questions than answers. The ER doctors, along with the floor doctors, could only treat Britney's symptoms and would send her home when she was stable but thankfully, her pediatrician was steadfast.

I remain forever grateful to Britney's pediatrician, Dr. Bryan, who is both brilliant and humble. When everything was mysterious, he never doubted us, never gave up and never stopped searching for answers. He frequently asked about his other patient, Zachary, out of concern for how he was handling the stress. I am equally appreciative of nurse Jan. She became Britney's advocate; she knew how to get appointments and results we needed and she knew how to take care of Britney. And, she was my rock! Jan took care of me when I didn't think I needed to be cared for. Together, they were the calm and steady support we needed, the reasonable during the unreasonable and always, they were a force to be reckoned with. They fought for Brit. They listened to her, got to know her and loved her. I was glad they were on our side.

Through all the stress that comes with illness, Britney worked very hard and made remarkable progress dealing with AS. She was learning to adapt in a world that most of us call normal. In reality, her world was anything but normal, even for a child without AS. Academically, she was light years ahead of her peers and socially, she was on track to attend a typical kindergarten class. A cloud of apprehension surrounded us medically but school wise, we felt an abundance of optimism.

Britney was excited about kindergarten because she wanted the same teacher who taught her brother and that became her motivation to succeed. If she could learn to adapt to the sights, sounds, smells and behaviors of other kids, she could be mainstreamed into a typical classroom. She was promised her favorite teacher if she could become less rigid and control her behaviors-rocking, head banging, flapping her hands and so on. She did it! She met every milestone and would be starting kindergarten as a regular student in a regular classroom. Zach had a full social schedule, was busy with all the extras that come along with elementary school and was cruising along just as steadily as he always had.

Even with this new normal, Britney developed more worrisome symptoms. In addition to sporadic fevers, joint swelling and pain, she was having more trouble urinating. She sometimes went three to five days without emptying her bladder and we were making biweekly visits to the doctor, fearing her bladder could burst. No one wanted to hurt her, but they had to catheterize her to give her relief. She would kick, scream and upset the entire office from the time we walked in until it was over. Then, Dr. Bryan would carry her to get stickers. These outbursts were not fair to anyone, but no one ever complained, and they treated Brit with love and compassion. One day, nurse Jan said, "You can learn to do this yourself". We all knew Britney would tolerate anything better if it came from me and if she had to suffer through it, I could step up and do my part.

Britney was lying on the table with her perfect little French braids and cherub face and I remember thinking, *"Will she look back on this and think that I tried to harm her? Will she know I had to do it? Will she know how hard it was to have to do it"?* That was the first invasive procedure that I learned to do to my daughter.

Any child going through all of this scary stuff would be overwhelmed and expected to lose control. I couldn't fathom what it was like, even as an adult, and to have sensory and processing issues exacerbating it all seemed beyond brutal. I wanted Brit to have an out, a safe place at home.

At home, Britney was allowed to have outbursts but only in her room. Mostly, she had meltdowns after extended social interactions or medical procedures. By that time, I knew how to help her decompress. She would jump off her bed ten times every night. Then I would press her joints, each one eight times, and then I'd roll her in a blanket and lay on her for two minutes.

On a good night, we wouldn't lose count and she would settle in for a restful sleep but those were few and far between. Having Asperger's syndrome meant Brit didn't sleep well, as most kids on the spectrum don't. Our alarm system would alert us if Britney tried to go outside during the night. She thought digging in the dirt, no matter the time, was a great idea.

All of these extra steps became our new normal and our lives settled into yet another routine. By the end of Britney's pre- kindergarten year, her constant urinary tract infections had affected her kidneys. Her doctors began to talk about dialysis and other possible interventions. Medically, we were all stumped but we weren't panicked because we thought she would outgrow it. She was active between episodes and she looked healthy. It was easy to forget the rough spots and settle in with the good ones.

Chapter 4

I liked my kindergarten teacher. Well, mornings were tough but I liked her in the afternoon; in fact I wouldn't want to leave school. Kindergarten was a really fun time. I had a friend, Faith. We would talk the entire time. We thought we were quiet but looking back, I'm sure we were not. If I behaved, I got to go up to the loft at nap time. They had books up there so it was super cool to be up in the loft. Every day after lunch, I had a sensory break and it was kind of fun. The sensory room had a huge peanut shaped ball and I could pretend it was a horse. There was a big rodeo barrel full of foam and the teacher's aide would roll me around. The trampoline was fun until they upgraded it to a safety trampoline with handles...then it wasn't nearly as much fun. Our class learned new dances. One was called the Tooty Tata. Some dances were okay, but the Tooty Tata was mortifying. We learned vowels, ABC's and numbers that was boring. At least at the end of the day the teacher would read us The Magic Treehouse. It was all about history and it took us back in time. That kind of story was fiction, but it was factual and it entertained me. I still like things that are factual.

I don't remember a lot about being sick. I remember getting fevers and some urinary tract infections. What I don't actually remember is the pain mostly just the aching. Things are much simpler when you are little. I think I don't remember because I choose not to. I remember a really high fever and I thought I was in a computer game. The room was swaying and everything was dream like.

—Britney

As Brit was promised, she started kindergarten with Mrs. Mc. As far as her school days had gone, it was the easiest first day so far and, when it was all said and done, the easiest first day of any of her school years. Brit had visited Mrs. Mc's classroom many times when Zachary was in kindergarten and several times during the previous year so, she was familiar with her surroundings. Her teacher had been teaching for over twenty years and had seen it all so Brit wasn't a huge challenge to her. The fact that Britney loved her so much went a long way but still, she did struggle with getting over-stimulated and the long hours with kids her own age wore on her. Had she been healthy and physically up to the challenge, I'd have made her stick it out because, as I became famous for saying, "It was good for her". However, I respected her teacher's opinion, the school nurse's opinion and our diagnostician's opinion so I listened, and we decided Brit needed a break halfway through her school day. With one sensory break a day, Britney flourished.

After a few weeks, she was not only on track, but she had made a friend. Things seemed to actually be stabilizing as far as keeping her mainstreamed in a normal classroom. We still had ARD meetings but her IEP (individual education plan) was pretty plain and simple. It focused on her social skills because she had no needs educationally, being that she was miles ahead of most children her age academically. Brit's IEP for the entire year was to say hi to one of the support staff as we walked by in the morning. Brit loved Mrs. D, but she didn't have any desire to say hello to anyone, especially in the mornings. Twelve years later when Brit graduated in the top percentage of her class, multiple academic cords around her neck and the National Honor Society stole proudly worn with her graduation gown, she turned to Ms. C and said, "I'm probably the only student to graduate with this many awards and medals but I never did say hi to Mrs. D. I am graduating high school, heading to Texas A&M University and I never completed my kindergarten IEP". As she said this and grinned she looked a whole lot like that stubborn little five-year old girl with the same tilt to her chin that she had every morning when she walked past Mrs. D and didn't say good morning.

As far as Britney's behavior, kindergarten was relatively uneventful with the exception of any interaction with the school's mascot or any assembly in the cafeteria. Once again, I wanted her to try to get used to it but we decided to make a few exceptions and looking back, I'm so grateful we did. This didn't just help Britney to cope, but it also brought her into contact with Ms. C, the school nurse, and that would be a relationship that grew and lasted over the years. Ms. C became Britney's strongest advocate in the school setting, one of her most trusted friends and one of my biggest supporters. She shared her family with Brit and her family shared in all the ups and downs that came Brit's way. They were cheering her on when Ms. C presented Britney's high school diploma and they once again had a front-row seat as we gathered one last time to honor Britney and say our goodbyes.

As uneventful as her kindergarten year was academically and behavior wise, her health was still declining. Brit started to show some mild seizure activity, her bladder issues were increasing and her kidney issues were still a mystery. All of this, on top of the bouts of constipation and clean outs, were getting more and more frequent. We could see that each day was becoming more of a challenge for her. Because we knew that her fevers were not caused by anything contagious, she was allowed to attend school as long as she was able and most of the time, she pushed herself to make it at least part of the day. Some days, it was so hard for her to walk that her classmates would push her in a rolling chair and by the time the winter weather caught up with her, she was occasionally using a tiny wheelchair.

There were multiple hospital stays, several ER visits and weekly doctors' appointments but I still thought that by next year, things would be better and she would go on to the next grade a healthy, normal six-year-old. That kind of thinking is what carried us through because we never lost sight of our goal and we truly believed we were going to get there. Every year we would think the next would be better and every year, after it proved us wrong, we'd hope that the next one would be better. Hope is a good thing and something we should all hold on to but hope can become detrimental when it clouds your reality.

As Britney finished out her kindergarten year, aside from her health, things were going so smoothly that my reality was more cloudy than ever. Had I known what the next few school years would be like, I'd have seen nothing but storm clouds with Britney most definitely being the eye of the storm. Leaving kindergarten would mean leaving this school and advancing to the next elementary level, which was first through fifth grade. I knew it would be a change for her, and I expected a challenge, but our one saving grace was that the school nurse, Ms. C, was moving to the new school with us.

Brit said goodbye to kindergarten but not to Mrs. Mc. Mrs. Mc stayed in both my kids' lives and continues to be a part of Zach's. I will forever be grateful for the continued relationship my kids have with her. She's been there to cheer them on and support them since Zach's first day of kindergarten.

That summer Brit was still battling health issues but didn't mind because she had found a new love in the form of our public library. She would take a box, not a bag, and fill it with books. Only not books from the children's section or even the young adult's section. She went straight to the science books and pulled every volume she could find on Newton's laws of gravity.

She found it fascinating and loved to educate us all even though we didn't find it remotely interesting. After listening to her try to educate other disinterested five-year-olds, I made a deal with her. If she wanted to read her science textbooks, she had to read one children's book first and, she and Zach had to pick a book on CD that they could both agree on to listen to in the car. She was not happy but settled on *The Magic*

School Bus books because she said at least she was learning something and it wasn't all fake.

So that was our summer, some of it in the hospital and some of it at home, but all of it consisted of learning more about gravity than any of us cared to know.

Chapter 5

First of all, first graders don't act much different than kindergartners. I didn't like going to a new school and everybody knew it. I didn't mean to scream every day but the cafeteria was right inside the front doors and I hated the smell. Plus, there were fifth graders walking in the same door and some of them didn't know what deodorant was.

So, you can understand why I hated walking in in the mornings. Plus, by now I always felt sick, like I was going to throw up, and the smells just made it worse but I didn't know how to say that. We did learn more and my teacher would let me read books way above first grade level. I really liked that because I could learn from them but I was getting sicker and I just wondered why did God waste this brain on this body?

—Britney

Our school district brings in a psychologist to give unbiased evaluations of the children, with special needs, and this was the year Brit was scheduled for her next evaluation. The doctor was given no information about Britney because it was important that he had no preconceived ideas. Still, Ms. C felt that she should warn him that Brit likely wouldn't go into the room without her, and if forced, there was a good chance she would act out. He assured Ms. C that he'd been doing this for a long time and he was confident that he would be able to handle Britney. He was wrong; Ms. C was in attendance when he started Brit's evaluation.

I guess I need to explain that as much as she advocated for Brit, and as good as she was at caring for all of the students, Ms. C didn't like any kind of confrontation or any stressful situations. Anytime we took Britney into a new situation, we knew to expect the unexpected. If Britney was going to be questioned, you could bet on the fact that her answers would be straightforward, brutally honest and sometimes needing explanation from a knowing adult. In this case, Ms. C was the reluctant, but knowing, adult and before it was over she was spitting out explanations and trying to make sure the doctor didn't think Brit was being raised by an army sergeant.

The psychologist tried to play some small games with Brit but she wasn't buying into it and told him so. He asked her if it would be okay to ask her some questions and she said yes. His first question was that he wanted to know what she liked to do on the playground. She said, "I don't like anything about it", so next he asked what she would choose to do if she could do anything she wanted to. Her reply- "I'd get under the slide, bite the kids ankles and bark at them". Then he asked "Well, why don't you do that then"? She answered, "Cause my momma would beat my bottom!"

After returning Brit to her classroom, Ms. C went back to the psychologist and, stumbling all over herself, explained that I didn't beat Brit at all but that she was disciplined. She was worried that he would take Brit literally but after a few words he looked up and said,"Call Britney's mother and tell her she's doing something right!"

I wish Britney had kept in mind that her "momma would beat her bottom" if she acted up, but apparently that slipped her memory. It definitely wasn't front and foremost in her mind when she decided she didn't want any part of a new school, a new classroom or a new teacher. Thankfully, her first-grade teacher had also been Zachary's so she was aware of Brit's medical struggles but, she also knew what I expected from my kids. She understood that Britney had some special needs but supported my efforts to push her limits and wanted to help her reach her full potential. Ms. Debbie was bright, cheerful and everything a typical six-year-old would want in a teacher. Not Britney! I would walk her to class before the other kids were released from the cafeteria in the mornings and Ms. Debbie would faithfully smile and offer a cheerful good morning. Britney saw nothing cheerful about a bright room that would soon fill up with many other six- year-olds and she made sure we all knew it. Sometimes she screamed and kicked, and sometimes she went in quietly, but by the time I made it to the front door, she had let loose on the teacher. Ms. Debbie was beyond patient with her and would take whatever Brit offered up until Ms. C could get down there and try to appease her. Sometimes this worked but more often than not, it didn't.

One morning, I made it out the front door and all the way home. I really thought that we had made some progress but then I got a call asking me to come back as Britney had decided that this wasn't her day. When I stepped into the first-grade hall, there were several teachers graciously smiling and as I walked into the classroom, I understood why.

Apparently, Brit had decided to wait until the other kids got to class to fully show her disapproval. She had crawled under a table, and with the other kids finding it all very interesting, Ms. Debbie had tried to coax her out. When she realized she wasn't having any success and the other kids were getting restless with the commotion, she had called for backup. The principal had been summoned and as he leaned down trying to console Britney, she grabbed his tie.

As I rounded the corner, I saw Mr. Jay on all fours and Brit had a firm grip on that tie all the while laying there silently looking like an angel, in her cute little outfit and braids, but with defiance written all over her face. She knew that if I came up there and she was screaming, she'd be in trouble so she stayed quiet. She thought that would keep her in my good graces. She hadn't given any thought as to who she had pinned down on the other end of that tie! When she saw my face, or feet, the tie was released! Thirteen years later, Mr. Jay, through laughter and tears, recounted this incident as he spoke at her funeral, per her directions.

I had learned to give her a chance to tell me why she was upset and not just react. Now, well into the second semester of first grade, she finally told me what the problem was. It wasn't Ms. Debbie's cheerful good morning and it wasn't all the kids in her classroom. The problem was; Britney was going through a Mary Poppins phase and the teacher next door looked like Mary Poppins! She wanted to be in that other classroom but I was determined that we had made it this far and she was going to stick it out in her own classroom. We came up with a plan and we made a chart so that Britney could see her progress. She had to walk quietly into the classroom five mornings in a row and, as a reward for her better behavior, she was allowed to visit Mary Poppins' classroom. Soon we were seeing success, and before long, she earned her very own desk in the coveted classroom.

Still, Britney's hospital visits were increasing. Her intestines were slowing down and she was losing her motility which caused severe constipation and was starting to cause malnutrition. We would be home for about 5 days and things would seem smooth but we would go for x-rays of her abdomen (KUB) on a weekly basis. Each time they would show that she was full of stool, Dr. Bryan would suggest we head to the ER and he would call ahead so they would be ready and waiting for her. He knew how hard this was on Britney and did everything he could to make the process as seamless and quick as possible. I would have to break the news to Brit who would get that deer-in-the-headlights look, and sometimes a little teary, but then pull herself together. Then we would grab our pre-packed hospital bag and leave for Dallas.

Britney knew what the routine was when we got there. Whereas before she would scream, now, she had become quietly resigned. She would bravely hold it together and stare at me with those big, dark eyes until the nurse walked in with the dreaded NG tube.

The first and only time I came close to fainting during a procedure was the first time I held her down while they ran a long tube up her nose, down her throat and into her stomach. The tube would stay in place for ten days to months on end. These tubes would irritate anybody's throat, but add sensory overload to the equation, and it results in constant gagging and choking. Sometimes it went on for so long and was so intense that blood ran out of her mouth and nose. Britney would rather have a long, complicated surgery than have that NG tube placed.

Years later, my aunt told me that one time she had come to the hospital with my parents to visit Britney. Before the elevator doors opened, they could hear Britney screaming as the nurses placed another tube. She said that, in all of her years visiting hospitals and ERs with her own children, she had never heard anything as anguished as Britney's cry. Until the day she died, she would tear up if you touched her nose, even playing around. At last count, Britney had fifty-eight different NG tubes placed.

Typically, the tube was placed in the emergency room and once the x-ray had been done to show it was in the proper place, they would take us to a room on the gastroenterology floor. This would be our home anywhere from ten days to six weeks. There, they would hook up a kangaroo pump to her NG tube and we would begin to pump gallon after gallon of liquid laxative into her stomach.

By the time Britney was eight, she could set the pump herself and dictate to the doctors and nurses the exact rate she could tolerate. Sometimes it would take over a week before we had any progress. Her belly would swell, she took no food or drink by mouth and I had to give her enemas, rectally, on top of what she was already getting. Brit had no control over her bowels so she was forced to lie in her bed in a diaper. Once the meds started working, Brit was thrown into a vicious cycle of horrible cramping, nausea and added retching. Then, if she was lucky, there would be a blow out causing a mess that resulted in being stripped of her gown and carried to the shower. As she showered I weighed her diaper, recorded it, put clean sheets on the bed and got her settled again. She would barely be back in the bed and it would start all over again, often more that twenty-five times a day. This would go on for weeks. She would be raw and depleted and we were both completely worn down. When it became evident that she was cleaned out and she had a clear KUB, we would get to go home. She'd go back to school, I would get caught up on housework and the cycle would start over again.

Brit and I often endured long stays, just the two of us, and the loneliness sometimes turned to hopelessness. It felt like everyone else's lives were moving on and we were living in a hospital far away from reality. We did know that people were thinking of her, and praying for her, and we did know that these times were hard on all of us, not just Brit and me. Still, after weeks of living in a hospital room with only the two of us, emotions sometimes took over reality and we felt very alone.

Some of our isolation was due to Brit's procedures and our desire to protect her privacy. Part of it was because more and more people were talking behind the scenes, forming their own uninformed opinions and making it increasingly hard for me to open up or share our every day life. Even as isolated as we were, the undermining comments being made were making their way back to me so, if I had decided to open up, I would have known every word was being judged. I will forever be grateful to our school district, and especially our school nurse, for becoming our constant support, encouragement and ultimately, our family.

As much as I felt alone in Britney's care, I am thankful for the part that some of my family and a couple of church friends played in Zachary's care. When you have a sick child one of the worst parts, as a mom, is that you can't be in two places at once. With Britney's special needs, she required me to be with her 24/7 and Zachary willingly gave up any time that Britney needed. The guilt of watching one child suffer and being so absent in my other child's life was often a heavy weight to carry around. Knowing that Zach was well cared for and given some stability by those who took him in as their own was a relief that I can't properly put into words.

These were exhausting, stressful times and to top it off, on one of our breaks home, I got my first of many calls from CPS. I'm sure that the calls made to CPS were made with the best of intentions but really, they were very detrimental to our family. I was already second-guessing myself and knowing that I was being watched and scrutinized only made it worse. Thankfully, Dr. Bryan and many of Britney's specialists called the social worker and they closed the case in less than an hour. This wouldn't be our last go-around with social services and I'm thankful that each time our caseworker was kind and seemed to have Britney's best interest at heart.

Here's the thing about CPS - they are confidential but, small towns aren't, and I knew who called CPS every time. My instinct was to run, go silent and not trust anyone to know the details of our every-day life but instead, I decided to be more transparent. I knew that by opening the door and letting people in, they would see the truth. Looking back, I know that I have the people who wrongfully doubted my ability to care for Britney, and falsely reported their accusations to authorities, to thank. Had they not pushed me to such fear of losing my children, all in the name of protecting our privacy, I wouldn't have become as transparent or developed relationships with so many in the school system. These teachers and staff became valuable assets and we were blessed to have them in our family.

Any of us parents can judge others, especially those who have to fight for their children's lives and micromanage every minute of every day. The thing is, we know you all are watching, we know you all are judging, we know you're talking behind our backs and to trump it all, we know that with any small suspicion our children can be taken away. The difference between parents of healthy kids, and parents raising medically fragile kids, is really quite simple. If you have a healthy child placed in a foster home, they run the risk of being mentally, emotionally and physically affected and that's nothing to be taken lightly. But, you take a medically fragile child and place them in a home with strangers, or even other family members who haven't lived your day-to-day struggles, and that child could pay with their life. Sadly, all of us who live most of our lives in doctors' offices and hospitals, have that hanging over our heads constantly. Thankfully, we had strong relationships with Britney's doctors and I knew if any problem arose, they would rectify it.

All of this played an enormous role in my anxiety. I should have been able to just focus on both of my children and, ultimately, on Britney's health. I shouldn't have had to fight anyone to get her the help she needed, or even dread mentioning any trip to the doctor or hospital, but that wasn't the case. The underlying tension between her father and me was always accentuated during Britney's bad times and I knew that it wasn't just him that I was up against. According to the church, it was my duty to be submissive to my husband in all things. While this is truly biblical, they distorted it in such a way that it equated to letting your husband think for you, speak for you, decide for you and do it all "as pleasing unto the Lord".

So, when Dr. Bryan would say it was time to head to the hospital, my first thought wasn't how hard it was going to be on Britney or myself. My first thought was, *"Oh no. I have to tell her father"*. For other women in the church, that would have meant "I have to *ask* my husband" but I had already gotten past that, much to the disapproval of my husband and the church.

With each trip to the hospital, the tension between her father and me was magnified though we never acted on it or let our children see it. Again, my job was, first of all, to be a wife by the church's standards and the more I poured into Britney, the less I poured into our marriage. I often felt guilty for that but my commitment to Britney outweighed anything else at the time. I felt that, as adults, we could work our way through whatever feelings of neglect we might have but how could a child work her way through those same feelings? Brit needed to know that I was all in and she would never have to do any of it alone.

Nothing in this world, or what our church family perceived to be my fate in eternity, was going to keep me from doing what I knew was best for my children. I realize any normal mother feels this way, and I realize that any couple will have their disagreements and tensions, especially while raising a sick child. The thing was, I wasn't just up against my husband in our disagreements. Had I pushed the envelope too hard, I would have run the risk of losing my children.

The leaders of the church had an innate ability to sniff out any weakness or issues in any of our lives and they had certainly sniffed out mine. I rarely went to a function without one of them approaching me to tell me that my husband wasn't being the husband and father they felt he should be and in truth, I felt the same. Had they encouraged me and tried to rectify the situation, their so-called concern may have been justified but in truth, they did just the opposite. While they complained to me about my husband, they took him aside and spoke of my independence, lack of submission and any reason they could come up with as to why Britney was as sick as she was. None of this was helpful and, in fact, did far more harm than good. There was enough underlying resentment between me and my husband and added opinions about our shortcomings were not helpful in any way, regardless of their subversive intentions.

When you're in the thick of this, you don't know which way is up and trying to balance the he said/she said in the middle of everything else only adds stress and anxiety. In a normal relationship the church, while playing a vital role in a godly marriage, would not have been the deciding factor on any given issue. The church should have been a place of refuge and peace and I know many that are but, not the one we were a part of. It was a place of rules and fear, especially for us women, and the thing I feared most would have likely been instigated by our church had I crossed the fine line of not being submissive enough. I was already pushing it, with one foot over the line, and I knew I had to watch my step. My biggest fear was losing my children, whether it be to death or having them taken away from me.

I knew that on his own, her father wouldn't have taken that step but I also knew the influence our church leaders had on every single one of us. They played such a vital role in all of our lives and, though it's embarrassing to admit now, we all wanted their approval and acceptance. For us, this came with added meaning because some of the church leaders were part of my own family. Some in my family had ill-conceived notions that something had been lacking in my childhood; therefore, I was coddling and babying Britney. They thought that really, there was nothing wrong with her and I was enabling her and seeking attention by letting her act out and, on top of that, exaggerating her symptoms. To this day, I still have trouble expressing anything physical or psychological going on with me without thinking I'm being overly dramatic or just seeking attention.

I was terrified that if they continued to drill this into her father's head, they would convince him it was best to keep Britney away from me. Had they been able to get him to that point, I would have been alone, without my kids, with no family and no life as I had known it. Discipline was strictly enforced in this church and part of my punishment would have been to be shunned by my family. I had seen instances where, though divorces were few and far between, the church always managed to get the upper hand and, whichever parent was in their favor, was awarded the children. This was always cause for righteous celebration because "surely the Lord had heard our cries and His will had been done". The fear of losing my children almost overtook the fear of losing our battle with Brit's health but thankfully, I never let it. Had they taken my children, no one would have had the ability to care for, or fight for, Britney like I did. She likely wouldn't have survived for any amount of time and she certainly wouldn't have received the tools she needed to cope in this world. Years later, I did lose my marriage and I did lose Britney, but neither came by me giving up or giving in without a fight. For now, I had too much on my plate and my main focus remained my children and Brit's serious health issues all while still trying to overcome Asperger's syndrome.

During this time, Britney had a new schedule, as it was constantly changing to accommodate her health needs. She went to school three days a week and was home for two. On the days she went to school, I would pick her up, bring her home and the clean-out regimen would begin. She had to swallow three oral laxatives and have two adult enemas every day. For a typical kid dealing with the trauma and pain each day would be overwhelming. For someone on the spectrum, the fear and pain, plus sensory overload, was excruciating.

Every day, she would come home knowing that I was going to have to hold her down and inflict pain all for her greater good. Most days, she would scream and run and I would have to chase her. On those days, Ms. C came and held her while I administered the enemas. When it was over, and she lay cramping on the floor, she would cry and apologize for fighting me. She was always reassured that she had done nothing wrong and it was I who owed the apology for having to do what needed to be done. Other days, she would lie quietly on her side with tears streaming down her sweet face, resigned to what she knew had to be done. Even then she would say, "It's okay, Momma. I know we have to do it". She would do whatever it took to not ever have to have an NG tube but still, before the week was out, we were sent back to the hospital and the process started all over again.

Through all of this, Britney kept her grades up and stayed connected with the other kids through her teacher and other school staff. Before we knew it, we were approaching the end of the year and her first-grade program was coming up. At first, the rehearsals went well but, when the practices were moved to the stage, she dug her heels in and wasn't having any of it. All of the first-grade teachers tried everything they could think of but none of them were having any success. It was Mrs. Debbie who decided to call her friend who was also Britney's former kindergarten teacher. It was decided that Brit and Mrs. Mc would do the program together and she would have never made it through that first-grade program had Mrs. Mc not sat on the floor behind the risers through the entire performance.

Soon it was time for field day. One of the best things about Britney was that she never let her diagnosis become her identity, so it didn't surprise anyone when she signed up to run a race and do the hurdles. That morning, we had to go for another KUB then I dropped her back at school while we waited for Dr. Bryan to call with the results. I had the printed films in my car and was pretty adept at reading them by now but hadn't looked at them because I didn't want to know. Britney had completed both of her races and was happily playing on the water slide when Dr. Bryan called my cell phone to tell me that one of her lungs was partially collapsed and we needed to head to the hospital. Britney's intestines were so full of stool it had pushed her diaphragm up and was compressing her left lung. I told Ms. C and she grabbed Brit's backpack. I wrapped Brit up in a towel and we headed home for one good shower before heading to the hospital. That was Britney's last day of first grade because trying to fix this latest development turned into a long hospital stay.

With school out for the summer, her doctors decided that we would stay in the hospital until we had a successful clean-out and Britney could eat without backing up. This meant another NG tube, another kangaroo pump and another round of laxatives and enemas. It took almost two weeks to get her cleaned out and, when she was able to start eating again, nothing worked. She had no motility at all. She started filling back up and when she got to the point that she was vomiting her own stool, a surgeon was called in. He explained a relatively new procedure called the ACE procedure. He would remove Brit's appendix and reposition it under her belly button. There was a tube coming out of her appendix, accessible through her navel and another tube, coming from the appendix, positioned in her lower intestine. We would be able to access through the belly button, with a catheter, and flush laxatives through her appendix and into her small intestine.

Britney came out of surgery with a large incision and a button where her navel used to be. We were used to tubes, needles and pumps but seeing a plastic button protruding out of your child's stomach is a lot to take in. I can only imagine what it was like for Britney but the fact that it was only supposed to be temporary, was some consolation to her. Little did I know that that button wouldn't be permanently removed until her spirit had left her body and I bathed her for the last time. I got some satisfaction from removing that button and seeing her belly with no foreign objects for the first time in twelve years. I suppose we should be grateful for that button. It worked for a full six months until her body threw us another curve ball.

Chapter 6

Well first of all, I hated second grade! The kids weren't getting any smarter and I wasn't being challenged. On the days I went to school, I made sure they all knew I didn't want to be there. Ms. C would try to give Momma a break and walk me to class but she didn't weigh very much and I'd just drag her in the opposite direction. I only went to school 2 days a week because I was getting sicker. I wasn't very nice to my teacher but, she finally figured out, that I liked being put at a desk away from other kids. She thought she was giving me consequences but really I just liked it."

—Britney

Before Britney's second-grade year, we spent most of the summer in the hospital. We were trying to figure out her motility issues but not having much luck. We were consistently flushing through the new button but that wasn't the solution we were aiming for. Still, we had found a rhythm and were able to go home with a lot of new equipment and continue the regimen. Because of all we had to do each day, Britney was enrolled in the homebound program. She attended school two days a week and had school at home three days a week with a homebound teacher. Until now, Brit had kept up with her work on her own but eventually, attendance would become an issue so we got ahead of it and enrolled her. We thought this would be temporary but Brit stayed enrolled in this program until she graduated high school. This meant longer ARD meetings, not just covering her AS, but also her health issues. I never attended one of these meetings alone. Ms. C was at every single one of them advocating for Britney as much, or more, than I was.

On Britney's homebound days, I started working mornings at my dad's medical clinic. Britney would go with me and lie on a pallet under my desk to do her school work or read. I was still determined to push her social skills so, I would put her at the front window to say hello to the patients and ask them to sign in. She hated it, but she did it, and she looked really cute doing it. So cute, that the elderly patients would talk to her and some went so far as to tell her their symptoms. She still looked just as cute when she would announce the remedy to any of their bowel issues or let them know that she didn't pity them for any of their ailments. None of them had suffered like she had and since she saw no need to complain about it, she didn't think they should either. Her no-nonsense attitude, and lack of tactful filter, cured many of those patients and they left with a smile.

There seemed to be a pattern forming and each year between October and February, Britney would struggle. The inflammation in her joints and fevers would develop, along with random infections that were hard to overcome, and there was always a bout or two of pneumonia. This year was no different except this time, when the inflammation started, we were sent to an immunologist. As we waited at our first appointment, Britney went into respiratory distress right there in the waiting room. I didn't realize at the time how serious it was. I only knew that she was struggling for each breath and suddenly everyone was moving very quickly. It was the care and concern of the doctor and his staff that won me over. Britney, on the other hand, was won over by Dr. T's skills and his acknowledgment of her potential. He spent time going over Britney's interests with her instead of just seeing her illness. He got to know her as a person, not just a patient, so she had a new friend, not just another doctor.

Dr. T is responsible for two very important happenings in Britney's life. First of all he asked us to try an experimental shot that eventually slowed Britney's juvenile rheumatoid arthritis and completely wiped out her fevers. The shots were thousands of dollars each month but worth every penny. Most importantly, Dr. T introduced Britney to the Fighting Texas Aggies. For the next ten years, he would work hard to sway Britney to one day bleed maroon and covet that Aggie ring that he wore on his finger. He was the second person she texted when she got her acceptance letter to Texas A&M.

While Britney's fevers and joint issues improved with the shot, her GI issues were getting worse. She was spending more and more time in the hospital and having more and more NG tubes. No matter how resigned she was on the trip to the hospital, she could only hold it together for so long and the first mention of that NG tube would send her into a frantic meltdown. I didn't blame her. I wanted to meltdown myself and I can only imagine how much harder it was for her. It was a never-ending roller coaster and the low points were far outweighing the high points. We were both getting worn down and understandingly so. With no answers, no real plan and no firm prognosis, we didn't have much to go on. We kept hoping things would get better and we were both driven to do whatever we had to do to get to the other side of this. But, no amount of flushes, enemas or fasting made it any better and there seemed to be no end in sight.

Britney showed a tenacity and strength that was superhuman. She put up her share of physical fights but they couldn't compare with the battles she had to have been fighting in her mind. Through every uncertainty, unplanned trips to the hospital, bad reports and disappointment, she only had one constant. That was me, and, I was fading fast. I can confidently say that, in those early years, Britney never saw me falter. She never saw my struggles with doubts, fear, uncertainty, exhaustion or overwhelming guilt for her having to go through this. Not only did I have the guilt of not being able to help her but at the time, it was assumed that her disease had come from me. I carried the gene for an autoimmune disease and we had all, including her doctors, assumed that she had inherited whatever this was from me. I had to put my shame aside because she deserved my full focus to be on her health. My goal was for us to beat this and for her to never doubt my support or the privilege it was to be by her side. I didn't want any of my weaknesses to become her worry. I was determined to walk every step with her and whatever adversity she faced. If I could have possibly made her fight my own personal fight, I would have.

I wish I could have taken the IVs, NG tubes, enemas and procedures for her. I wish I could have taken her pain and anxiety or walked the bulk of this road for her, but I couldn't. I could, however, walk beside her every step of the way and any hardship that she had to endure, I wanted to endure with her. If she didn't eat, I didn't eat. If she couldn't leave her hospital room for weeks or months, I didn't leave the room. If she couldn't go outside for weeks, I didn't either. If she was covered in stool or blood, being right beside her meant that I was too. Truly it was a privilege and an honor to be beside her but the fact that I couldn't take it all away was gut-wrenching.

As we went through each episode, I had to shut my emotions down and run on adrenaline. My stomach stayed in knots, my head pounded and my heart physically hurt. During the times we were lucky enough to be back home, the previous episode haunted me with anxiety during the day and nightmares at night. There was no time to stop and deal with this because we were already gearing up for the next go-round. I was so focused on being there for her, trying to make up lost time with Zachary and keeping our home running as smoothly as possible that I missed the subtle signs that my body was showing me. The more warning signs that my body gave me, the more I pushed back. When you stuff your emotions, they become physical and when they become physical, your body reacts. When you're emotionally and physically depleted, things can come to a screeching halt-and they did!

There was another unexpected trip to Dallas, another NG tube, another clean out and no food or drink for Britney. Typically, I was prepared with a packed suitcase, snacks and some cash but this time I truly thought we would be in and out. I was prepared for a short stay and it quickly became apparent that we were going to be there for another long haul. I had only brought a bag with a few changes of clothes, two granola bars and a few necessities but no cash. Because Britney wasn't allowed to eat, I wouldn't either but, after a couple of days, I did sneak into the bathroom and wolf down a granola bar. That only lasted two days. I couldn't sneak down to the cafeteria and leave Brit alone with her combined fear, anxiety and Aspergers. Had I done that, my absence would have resulted in chaos being that she could remove any tube, needle or medical device in seconds. She would also turn anything she could reach including emesis basins, IV bags and IV poles into weapons of mass destruction with her favorite targets being nurses and most especially, GI doctors. To top it all off, I had no cash and there are no free rides for parents in the hospital.

While Britney couldn't take anything by mouth, she was being sustained with IV fluids and some nutrition through her NG tube. I, on the other hand, was not. With ninety—six hours of constant clean outs consisting of hourly trips to the bathroom, bed changes, showers and extensive cleanup along with gagging and retching on her NG tube, we had little to no sleep at all. By day four, I knew I was in trouble. I had a horrible headache and I was dizzy, clammy and nauseous. I called my husband and after telling him how sick I was, he planned to come the next day and bring me some money. By the time he got there, and I made it down to the cafeteria, everything was buzzing and I could barely order my food. I have no memory of paying for it. I don't know how I made it out to the picnic tables but, thinking that the fresh air would clear my head, I managed to stumble out there and it only got worse. I know I had a few sips of my drink and a few bites of my food before I started violently vomiting. That went on for a while but, when things quit spinning, I staggered back to Britney's room where I immediately became sick again. I have no memory of what happened after that but Brit told me later that I was shaking and the nurses came in the room to take my blood pressure and assess me. I woke up several hours later in the ER, of the adjoining adult hospital, and my skirt was missing. I lay there for a few minutes, realizing that Britney was probably scared to death and I needed to get back to her. So, I pulled off my hospital bracelet, wrapped a blanket around my waist and walked barefoot back to the children's hospital next door. When I walked in Britney's room she was sitting up calmly in her bed.

After I had been taken to the other hospital, my husband called my dad who, in turn, sent my mom to Dallas with meds to control my symptoms. My husband left when my mom got there. Britney was happy being with her grandmommy and she happily gave me a run down on my symptoms and what the nurses had done for me. Her only concern was that she'd rather me not vomit so loud next time. She also said that when the nurses were concerned that I was having a seizure, she informed them that I wasn't and was just dehydrated and hungry. She was, of course, right.

This was the wake-up call that I needed because we would spend the next several months in the hospital and I needed to take better care of myself for her sake. We got to go home for a little bit, but it was short-lived, and soon we were back at our home away from home.

That stay, Britney was admitted into the hospital before Halloween and she wouldn't be released until some time in January. If it hadn't for the friendships formed with nurses, I would have gone insane. Britney, on the other hand, when she could block out the medical parts, didn't mind at all. Holidays in the hospital are as special as they possibly can be and the volunteers go above and beyond. It was extra special for Brit because we didn't celebrate religious holidays in our home, being that they were considered pagan by the church we were a part of. Brit loved the crafts, the treats and all the special events that went on during the holidays. After so many stays, she had bonded with some of her nurses and was more comfortable and relaxed than she had been in the past. This allowed me to leave the room when I needed to and one evening as I came around the corner, the Christmas carolers were standing in front of Britney's room. She had pulled her IV pole out as far as the cord would allow so that she could open the door. She was requesting every Christmas song she could think of, all the while, grinning and dancing. Brit spent most Thanksgivings and Christmases in the hospital but to her, they were happy memories. Although we celebrated Thanksgiving, and we always had a good time with our family, Christmas was a different story.

Those holidays were spent at church camp where the word *Christmas* was not mentioned without a derogatory tone. Our children did get to play with other children during the day and, while Zach enjoyed this, Brit hated it. Twice a day, there were services held that lasted several hours and sometimes lasted in to the wee hours of the morning. Our children were expected to sit through this and, while Zach passed the time reading or drawing, Brit made it a point to let everyone in the chapel know how much she despised every minute. I'll always be a little proud of her for that.

Most years, like this one, she didn't have to endure camp because she was in the hospital. And, that's where we were when shortly after Christmas, she started to decline and her bloodwork showed infection. The clean outs through her button and her NG tube weren't working and her other organs were starting to show the effects. Soon after the new year, things started progressing and we were feeling pretty hopeless. Because of the holidays, a new GI doctor, Dr. S, was on call and he ended up being one of Britney's many blessings. He suggested that we get a surgery consult and discuss the option of an ileostomy because he felt that we could put an end to a lot of her issues. He felt that if she was able to bypass her colon, her constipation issues would greatly decrease and the hospital stays, along with the dreaded NG tubes, would be much fewer and further between. Why her other GI doctors let her suffer for so long without offering this option, I will never understand. But, we will always be grateful for Dr. S stepping in and doing what he felt was his very best for Britney.

The surgeon, Dr. M came into our room at four o'clock the next morning turning all the lights on and booming "Good morning!" Britney was *not* impressed and was not having any of it but, I trusted him. I was grateful when he suggested leaving Brit's colon intact because that would give her a much better chance of being reattached, and getting rid of the ileostomy, in the future. Dr. M was leaving on holiday vacation with his family that day so he scheduled the surgery for five days later when he got back, but by late that evening, Dr. S. knew that we couldn't wait. He called Dr. M who was eight hours into his trip. Dr. M turned around and, with his entire family in tow, drove back to the hospital to take Brit into surgery in the wee hours of the morning. The entire floor was disrupted as I lay on Britney and we were wheeled down to the OR with her kicking and screaming.

That was the first of many, many times that I got to put on a sterile suit and accompany her into the OR for everyone's safety. The first of eight times I would hold her down, reassuring her that everything would be okay, until the anesthesia took effect and she would go limp.

I was no stranger to waiting rooms but sitting in this empty, silent one made the minutes drag on. After several hours, Brit's father arrived and a short while later we were both called back to see her. This was a huge mistake because, up until now it was always just me in recovery, and as Britney woke up she was not happy that her dad was in the room. It threw her completely off guard, as he had never been in recovery before, and when she saw him, she thought she must be dying because in her mind, why else would he be there? Britney's frustrations escalated and his frustration mirrored hers. That's an extremely hard situation to try to navigate when you're the mom who's trying to do what's best for her child but, you're also the wife who's trying to be submissive to her husband. On one hand, I was trying to sooth Brit's screaming and calm her fears of having her dad in the room. On the other hand, I was trying to imagine how he was feeling, but at the same time, trying to ignore the growing tension in that room. Thankfully, many of the nurses in recovery had been down this road with us and they knew the underlying cause of Brit's fears and frustrations so, they asked everyone to clear the room and left me in there, alone, to soothe Brit.

Because of Brit's well-known adverse reaction to anesthesia, the team was well acquainted with her needs. They had decided to try to keep her sedated to give me time to process what I was going to see. Brit had obviously thrown a kink in those plans so the anesthesiologist administered a sedative to put her back to sleep. Once she drifted off, the nurse pulled back the sheet and, though we were veterans in the medical world, nothing could have prepared me for what I saw. Brit's little body already had a nasty scar on her lower abdomen from the ACE procedure but now on her left side she had a small hole. Just a hole, nothing covering it up and nothing coming out of it. On her right side there was a stoma; a small portion of angry red intestine hanging out of her tiny little belly. Over the next week, I would learn how to care for Brit's stoma, seal a bag to her belly for her stool to empty into and pull mucus out of that little hole that was known as a mucus fistula.

Over the next six years, I would become an expert at all things ostomy and, while Britney never laid eyes on her bag, she amused herself by learning how to send a geyser up at my face as I was changing it. Later, the school staff went above and beyond, by asking me to please let them help me by emptying her bag, because I was going up to the school every two hours to do it. She rewarded them by eating anything she could to try to gross them out the next day. Spaghetti and blue Gatorade, when seen floating in an ostomy bag, bear a shocking resemblance to blue worms swimming. This made her laugh and brought some much-needed amusement to her day.

Soon the school year was coming to an end. The ostomy was doing its job and things seemed to be looking up. We were looking forward to a lazy summer and hoping for a better start to Britney's third-grade year.

Chapter 7

I don't want anyone to wear black at my funeral and I don't want flowers, I want hay. I don't want any preaching, especially long preaching, but if they try maybe they'll be allergic to the hay. I want a blue casket, no pink. But really, I want to be cremated and you can buy a bag for that on Costco's website. No sad songs, just Reba!

—Britney

Early in the summer, Ms. Cindy found out that Britney was going to be in her class for the third grade. She wanted to get to know Brit over the summer so she made the effort to spend a lot of time with her. She had seen me drag Britney past her own classroom, over the past two years, and wanted to make the next year easier for everyone involved. Her efforts paid off and when school started in the fall, Brit and Zach walked into school together for the very first time.

Up until now, I had made a conscientious effort to make sure that Zachary had as normal of a school experience as possible. It was important to me that he wasn't depended on to calm Britney's outbursts or do anything that a typical brother wouldn't have to do. At home, he was already bearing the burden of a medically dependent sibling and though her outbursts were few and far between at home, that wasn't the case in the school setting. I didn't want that to carry over into his day with his friends.

In previous years, each morning I would pull through the drop-off line and Zach would bounce out of the car and into the school. He was the type who said hi and stopped to hug everyone he knew; the complete opposite of his sister. After he walked into the school, I'd pull into a parking spot, give him time to get to his classroom and haul Britney out of the car. Once I managed to get her out of the car, anyone within hearing distance knew we had arrived and I didn't want Zach to be embarrassed. He had always put his sister before himself and had he been in hearing distance, he wouldn't have been able to ignore her needs. He would have swallowed his own embarrassment to make sure she was okay and would have worried about her the rest of the day. Watching your children walk into school together is something most parents take for granted but for me, it was a huge milestone. I was so thankful for Ms. Cindy's efforts but they didn't stop there. This year, like the others preceding it, would hold its own challenges and Ms. Cindy went above and beyond to show Brit how much she cared for her and how much she wanted to help her to succeed.

Britney's ileostomy was doing its job, and the dreaded clean outs were becoming more of a memory, but soon, new problems appeared. She kept developing dumping syndrome and each time would require hospitalization for dehydration. She also started showing signs of malnourishment and the problems with her kidneys resurfaced. This resulted in repeated hospital stays and we soon found that Brit wasn't absorbing nutrients or the fluid volume that she needed to keep herself hydrated. We started bi-weekly visits from home health to administer IV fluids and some medicines. Each week, Britney dreaded the IV needle pokes, blood draws and multiple blown veins. After months of this unpleasant regimen, it was decided that she would have a port placed, home health would access it and after a couple of weeks, I would learn to access it too.

Britney's port was placed low on her ribs and for the six years she had it, it never ceased to be uncomfortable. The typical place for a port is in the artery right on top of your collar bone but Brit had had so many central lines, that there was too much scar tissue. Having the port freed up both of Britney's hands when she was getting her fluids twice a week but it rubbed on her ribs so badly that she couldn't stand up straight.

The fluids helped but soon she was needing them three and four times a week and it was decided that it was time for me to learn to poke that needle through her skin and into her port. It took me longer than I would like to admit to make myself do it but, by the time she had her first port removed, I had accessed it over five hundred times. Accessing a port is a tedious, sterile procedure and staying hooked up to an IV pump for hours each day is disruptive and consuming especially for a child.

Britney, as with any aspect of her diagnosis, didn't let it consume her and continued on with her every day life. We would time her access to right before the homebound teacher got there and let her fluids run for the length of her lessons. There were times that she wore a special backpack with her pumps and IV fluids and she went to school or on field trips that way. She didn't let her diagnosis become her identity and I didn't either. We just pushed on, ignored the stares, appreciated the support and lived life to the fullest of our abilities. It truly was her attitude, and not just her abilities, that got us through and I was proud to follow her lead and live in her shadow. Britney's health was being managed and she seemed to be doing better socially, even making a few friends, so we settled into our new routine and started to breathe a little easier.

Just as we were getting comfortable, things took another turn as Britney's motility slowed and her kidneys started acting up more consistently. While they were not failing, they weren't functioning as they should and this resulted in some concern and many hospital stays. When these episodes occurred, it was very uncomfortable for her as it caused a lot of swelling which, in turn, caused added stress to her inflamed joints. Also, the fluctuation of the ten to fifteen pounds of extra fluid buildup was causing major damage and harm to her other organs. Once again, we found ourselves living at the hospital a lot more than we were living at home.

More time in the hospital was discouraging enough and to add to it, we didn't have a definite diagnosis. That left us with no real plan and no prognosis to wrap our minds around or prepare for. Brit wasn't following any of the patterns of the illness she had been diagnosed with and it seemed that with every new symptom there was a new mystery to solve, a new organ that was affected and more invasive testing. One continual test after another was a lot for any child to bear but nothing could have prepared us for the brutality she was going to have to face for the motility testing. Of all the tests that Britney had, it was the most harrowing to her and would become the one that haunted her most. This was the first, but wouldn't be the last time she had to endure this horrible procedure.

Motility testing, at best, is invasive. But truly, it is an invasion of your personal being, your mental resolve and a violation of your dignity. To your typical child it is overwhelming, but to a child on the spectrum it is unbelievably brutal. The process has since been improved but at that time, the testing lasted for several days and required a hospital stay. The first day consisted of an extensive clean-out with no food or drink. The next morning, she was taken into the OR where there was a tube placed down her nose and into her stomach and extended to her ileum. Next, a tube was threaded through the stoma of her ileostomy where it was met with a tube coming up from her rectum. This is a time-consuming process because there are hundreds of probes on each tube that have to be embedded into the lining of her digestive tract. One of the major hurdles in this process is trying to keep her from pulling out all the tubes as she's waking up from the anesthesia. Long before she's aware of her surroundings, she starts choking and gagging on the tube running down her throat and this typically continues until the tube is removed three days later.

Brit would reposition herself many times until she found a position that lessened the gagging and choking but it was usually an awkward one that resulted in me standing and holding her head at a certain angle all through the night and most of the next day. As the years went by, we knew to be prepared for no sleep, lots of messes, loss of dignity and many tears but our first time, we were flying blind. Neither of us were prepared for, or could have possibly imagined, what we would go through even if we had been warned.

Day two of the motility testing consists of being flat on your back for eight hours which does nothing to help with the gagging. You have to lie as still as you possibly can and you're hooked up to all kinds of monitors. There are many wires threaded up through each tube and each wire is connected to a specific probe. They bring a computerized machine to the bedside and the tech connects each wire to its specific port. This allows every inch of Britney's GI tract to be tested to see if it is functioning right, specifically for motility.

So, as I said, Brit was lying flat on her back and for the first couple of hours, her only job was to lie still. If she moved at all, any time during the test, the time would have to start over. I believe they brought in pudding for her to eat so they could test the progression of it as it moved through her esophagus. A couple of hours later, they started administering a stimulant which caused severe cramping, nausea and bloating. It should have started everything moving but, in Britney's case, she lay there cramping and hurting with no success for hours. Then it would suddenly come gushing out in a river of loose stool and, in no time, we'd both be covered. All the while she could not move a muscle and if you can imagine being covered in poo from the back of your neck to your ankles, being still was unimaginable. I had to try to scrape the slimy mess out from under her without moving her. I had stool smeared from my thighs to the bottom of my feet and dripping from my elbows. The stench was unbelievable but I tried to keep my face pleasant and swallowed the bile creeping up in the back of my throat. I never thought it was gross or nasty because that was my baby girl and the only thing I could feel was pity for her. The diaper we had put on her, and the disposable pads protecting the sheets, did little to contain the flood and soon it was all over the floor. Wherever this stimulant coming out of her touched my skin, it caused it to burn. I can only imagine how it felt to her insides because it left her skin chapped and raw and just using a damp cloth would burn her skin even more. It was a vicious cycle watching her suffer through the cramping, be humiliated with the mess, lie there defeated while I cleaned her up then bravely start the process all over again.

This went on repeatedly for the remainder of the test and then she got to endure them pulling out the tubes with no sedation or numbing. Removing the tubes was a relief but she was limp and exhausted and the stimulant was still working so we had hours of cramping and messes to endure. Typically, things would slow down during the night and I'd get her showered, change her sheets and get her tucked back into bed where she would fall into an exhausted sleep. Once she was settled, I would get cleaned up and hope to sleep but I'd been running on adrenaline for the last forty-eight hours. Between the adrenaline and watching her suffer, sleep was a long ways away. About the time I'd start to drift off, it would be the nurse's shift change, so we were both awakened and our day of hospital life would start again.

Typically after having all these tests, you would have answers, hopefully a diagnosis and a plan for treatment. Britney was never typical and usually her tests were non-conclusive, meaning we would leave the hospital without a plan and more discouraged than when we got there. Even though we were years into this we still went into each hospital stay with hopes of answers and direction. It seemed that we rarely got them and on the few occasions that we took one small step forward, her body would throw another curveball and we were shoved three steps back. This first motility test was no different.

Once again, Britney was finishing up another school year with more days missed than attended. Still, she had kept up her grades and was one of the top students in her class. I knew that this year she regretted missing so much because she really loved Ms. Cindy but Brit blew it off by saying, "At least I didn't have to worry about lice!" Lice was rampant that year, in the school, and Britney was trying to find the blessing in all of her absence.

Even though Brit missed out on much of the school year, overall, this year was a turning point for her. She loved Ms. Cindy and Ms. Cindy loved her. With her constant encouragement and Brit knowing that she had her back, Brit blossomed on the days that she could attend. She started making friends, started communicating more and these improvements brought challenges of their own. Britney never felt like she was above anyone, or even smarter than the other kids, but she did feel the need to teach them when they got something wrong. Her correcting didn't just pertain to other kids; she felt the need to correct adults also. While she truly believed she was only helping out, sometimes her corrections came across as disrespectful or as a know-it-all.

Brit had long ago learned to watch me for cues during any social situation so we came up with a plan that made her correcting people a little more tactful. When someone would say something that Brit knew was incorrect, she would look at me. If I felt like it was appropriate for her to correct them, I would give her a subtle nod and she could explain whatever they had done or said wrong. We had to come up with a phrase to lead into her corrections. "You're wrong. That's not right" or a disgusted look were not appropriate. So we came up with a more tasteful way to lead into her corrections. Hence, the phrase "Well, actually" was born. That phrase followed Brit, and became one of the most memorable things about her, for the rest of her life.

There's not a medical professional, teacher, friend, relative, rodeo associate or college professor who can't tell at least one story of a time that they heard "well, actually" before Britney said something profound. Sometimes it still sucks the wind out of me when someone says "actually" but overall the words "well, actually" make me smile, almost like sharing a private joke with my girl.

Another blessing that Ms Cindy brought was that we had access to a pool and thankfully, she loved swimming as much as my kids did. The school year was over so Brit and Ms. Cindy built a friendship apart from school and that friendship lasted through the years. Swimming was something they both enjoyed, and health wise, Britney benefitted from it greatly. Swimming took all the pressure off of her joints and stimulated her bowels to contract where they had lost motility. Her quality of life improved over the summer and she flourished not only physically, but socially. It's a lot easier to focus on social skills when you're not dealing with pain and physical ailments.

Chapter 8

Animals tell you what they want by their actions. You don't have to figure out their words, or what they mean by their words, they just show you what they want. They are much less complicated than us humans.

—Britney

A new grade was beginning and we had a plan going into it. Britney had spent time with Ms. C's daughter, Cat, over the summer. Cat had watched Britney for me on a few occasions and had formed a bond with her. Britney felt so comfortable with her that she decided to educate Cat, and eight of her friends, on the birds and the bees. Apparently, Brit had learned quite a bit from an AARP magazine that she had picked up at her grandparents' house. She had gone into great detail educating them on the assorted diseases you could get from having sex. No doubt, her dissertation began with "Well, actually!" Knowing that the girls would soon be going into middle school, she thought they should be prepared for these things. She was nine years old and far too knowledgeable and accurate in her teachings.

Since Britney had finally found a friend in someone closer to her own age, it was decided that Cat would be the one to walk her to class on her first day of fourth grade. I walked her to the door and she happily trotted off with Cat. Years later, at her funeral, her fourth-grade teacher was quoted as saying, "I knew about Britney and knew about some of her struggles, but I'll never forget that first day of school. Cat had walked her to class and I remember she looked like an American Girl Doll. She was dressed in a little plaid skirt. She had big, dark brown eyes and her hair was French braided down each side of her head. She was quiet and respectful but I could see the intelligence in her eyes. She never asked to be treated differently and though she struggled with attendance, she was one of my top students."

By all appearances, the year started out great for Britney but behind the scenes, there were new subtle symptoms that were becoming hard to ignore. Brit had developed a pattern over the last few years and would get sick sometime around late fall and not improve until well into the spring. It looked like this year would be no different. She was still having bouts of dumping syndrome, some trouble with her kidneys and intermittent swelling. The swelling seemed to be exacerbated by her arthritis which was affected by the changes in the weather. In short, the cooler weather would set off a chain of events in Brit's body that had resulted in pneumonia the last two years. This year, she developed pneumonia three separate times over two months and Dr. Bryan felt that it was the result of the extra fluid retention.

Not only was Britney's pulmonary function showing signs of stress, but she began having cardiac symptoms for the first time. This resulted in two new specialists and two new pieces of equipment, the wheelchair and an oxygen tank. Britney did not enjoy any kind of added attention but people can't help but notice and stare at a child encumbered with equipment that is typical for seniors. Equipment that no child deserves to be familiar with, let alone burdened with.

Brit had never been bothered by any medical equipment, or any special accommodations that she needed in school, but the wheelchair and oxygen bothered her. As a parent, you know your child needs to follow the doctors orders but you have to take their feelings into consideration so, it was my job to weigh both options and come up with a compromise. We agreed to leave the oxygen in the nurse's office, and Brit would use it any time she needed it, but especially during lunch and several other scheduled times. As far as the wheelchair, she would use it for any trips outside the classroom but move around on her own in between. Her classmates took turns pushing her and there were always several waiting in line to have their turn.

Brit was still on the schedule of attending school two days a week and having her homebound teacher two days a week. This worked well because it gave her several full days of oxygen per week and by now, she was needing IV fluids at least three days a week. The constant needle pokes, more frequent doctors' visits and loss of stamina were starting to weigh heavily on Britney and for the first time, I could see some breaks in her resolve. One day, it all became too much and she asked me if she could just stop. I had always told her that when she got too tired, and things became too much, I'd honor whatever decision she made so we made an appointment to go see Dr. Bryan.

That was the first of many tough visits and though most of it is a blur, parts of it stick out in my mind like it was only yesterday. I can tell you exactly what he had on, what room we were in, how Britney's hair was styled and every other detail of that day. Jan, who had been his nurse since Britney was born, was in the room. Somewhere along the way, Jan had quit being the nurse and had become a trusted friend to both Brit and me. For me, she was more than just a friend; she was my most trusted and reliable support. So for the four of us to be in that room, as surreal as it was, it seemed right that we would all be together. Dr. Bryan told Brit he understood that she was tired of it all and she said yes, that she was sick of being poked, tired of being sick, didn't want to hurt anymore and was ready to be done. None of us could look at each other but Britney, when asked if she knew what would happen, calmly told us exactly what would be expected. "Without my fluids, I will dehydrate. My muscles will cramp and I'll get a bad headache. My blood pressure will change, and I may hallucinate, but then I should fall into a deep sleep. I'll probably have seizures but, my muscles could just be spasming, and after that, it shouldn't be much longer." She was matter of fact, calm and to the point. We have Asperger's syndrome to thank for that.

Where each step like this took an emotional toll on all of us looking on, it was all just facts to Britney. This was the first of many times we would walk this path. By following her lead, I learned to keep my emotions in check knowing that giving into them would only make things harder for her. All children think their moms are invincible and we moms, raising medically fragile children, are adept at playing this role. So thankfully, I was able to keep my face neutral as we headed home with Brit giving me strict instructions on how to carry out her funeral plans for the second time. This time, she still wanted to be cremated but would go with the blue casket if we insisted on burial. She decided there could be a little bit of preaching so everyone would "know I'm okay". She still wanted hay and was adamant that there would be no flowers. It was very important to her that Ms. C and I sit together to take care of each other. Driving down that road, little did I know we would be sitting side by side eleven years later, just as Britney had planned.

No matter what Britney was thinking and planning to do at this stage, my brain was working overtime to try to come up with any solution to keep my baby girl fighting for another day. When we got home, Brit settled in on the couch and seemed more peaceful and content than she had been in a long while. It seemed to be a relief to her to know that she had some control and I would support her. Only, I wasn't relieved and knew I had to find a solution. i needed find something that she found worth fighting for so she would think it was her idea to keep going.

Again, we didn't have Google back then and searching the internet for answers wasn't just a simple click away. I had seen a brochure for Wings of Hope but hadn't put much thought into it because, in our everyday world, I didn't think of Britney as *special needs*. Now I found myself frantically searching and trying to find all the information I could on this equine therapy organization. By the end of the day, I had found the phone number and printed all the paperwork we needed for Dr. Bryan to fill out in order for an instructor at WOH to do an assessment. I called Jan and told her about my plan. We agreed I would bring the paperwork to be signed the next day and we all hoped that this would change Britney's mind. I think we all went to bed that night feeling like we had a chance to make it happen.

The following morning I delivered the paperwork to Dr Bryan. He signed it and, the very next day, we were at Wings of Hope! There were no riders in the barn that day, no classes and no distractions. As we walked into the barn we were met by Ms. Julie and right away, Britney warmed up to her. I was not familiar with barn life so I had dressed Britney up in a cute little pink shirt and perfect braids that we had to take down in the first ten minutes in order to get a helmet on her. Then we were taken out to a pasture where about twenty horses came to greet us. Later, we learned this was highly unusual and that the horses typically ignored humans and chose to graze instead of socializing, but not today. Every one of them wanted their chance to nuzzle Brit and get as much attention as they could. Usually the instructor chooses the horse best suited for each rider but this time, the horse chose his rider.

Chocolate was a light gray, an almost white, gelding who was playful and loving but had a bumpy gait. Brit was warned that his unsteady walk could jar her joints and cause her pain but she loved him and wanted to give it a try. Chocolate had been born a chestnut color and matured into the light gray he was now. This bugged Brit to no end, because his name didn't fit him, but she loved that horse and for the first time in a while, she was smiling again. On the way home she couldn't stop talking about the horses and she couldn't wait to get to ride. I let her ramble on and on but reminded her that if she stopped her fluids, she wouldn't have the strength to ride; if she was even here at all. Years later, when she wrote a letter to Wings of Hope, she talked about that day and how "Momma manipulated me into living" but thanked them for giving her a reason to live and for later introducing her to her best friend.

Brit had partnered with Chocolate for four months and they were getting ready to compete in their first show. Chisholm Challenge is a competition between the therapeutic riding centers of Texas. It kicks off the Fort Worth Stock Show and Rodeo each year and is an unbelievable experience for the riders and those of us fortunate enough to get to watch them compete. This was her first competition but you wouldn't have known it because there were no nerves, just happy excitement, determination and confidence. Brit and Chocolate had a good run in Western Equitation but Chocolate decided he didn't need to back up so they fell out of first place. The ring steward shook Brit's hand and said that, had it not been for her horse, she would have won first place. Then, he told her that when she came back to win it next year, he wanted to shake her hand again. He got that chance the following year, only Brit was riding a different horse, and we have Chocolate to thank for that because, had he not acted up, she wouldn't have met Red.

Red replaced Chocolate for Britney's next event. Not only did he help her win that event, but he helped her face and conquer every fear and battle she encountered over the next seven years. He was her soulmate, her best friend, her most trusted confidant and the reason she wanted to live. Those of us who witnessed their relationship can't find the words to describe it. It seemed to be supernatural, ethereal, almost incomprehensible yet, pure and simple. Their's was a friendship and loyalty that surpassed human comparison and they had a love that few of us ever experience. It was a love that Britney had never, and would never, experience with any of us. I knew she loved me, her dad and her brother but she couldn't express it and wasn't comfortable showing it. It's important to know that Brit did show love through her actions, caring ways and concern for others but she was never at ease with affection. With Red, all of that changed.

I wish Britney agreeing to continue her fluids and loving Red would have turned her life into fairy-tale story but, while it did improve her outlook, her health continued to decline. Brit looked forward to her once-a-week dates with Red but missing him made her hospital stays even more miserable. Her instructors reached out with support, pictures of Red, encouragement and friendship. Before long, I realized Brit was starting to bond with her people and not just her equine partners. The relationships she formed with the people of WOH would become some of the strongest bonds and closest friendships she would ever have. Now, when she casually went over her funeral plans, she would include a special place for them to sit and, in addition to the hay and still no detested flowers, donations could be made to her beloved Wings of Hope.

While it is disturbing and unsettling to hear a child that young speak of their funeral plans as if they're planning their next birthday party, it's a conversation that comes up often. Children who grow up in the halls of hospitals, enduring procedures and operations that most adults never give thought to, are wise beyond their years. While we parents want to protect them, and ourselves, from any fear or uncertainties it's often our children who put things into perspective and make us face reality.

I always let Britney talk. I assured her that I would do exactly as she asked and then ended the conversation with platitudes and reassurance that she didn't have to worry about any of that. I'd listen calmly, with my brave mask on, stoically answering all her questions and agreeing with her ideas and plans. Often after she was settled and focused on other things, I would go outside and crumble. I rarely cried but I'd fight to breathe, punch a brick wall until my knuckles were scraped and lean against the house, often vomiting before I pulled myself together and went back inside. At home, I didn't remain calm only for Britney; I had Zach to consider also. He had enough on his plate without worrying about his momma and I wanted so badly to make things easier for him.

When we were in the hospital and had these discussions, I'd get her settled in with her crafts and go run up and down the stairs until I could barely breathe. When I knew I could get past the nurses station without panting, I would head back to her room, shower and settle in to my role of making the best of our situation. That was one thing that Brit and I always focused on.

"If we are going to have to be where we are and have to do what we are doing, we are going to do it the best it can be done. We are going to do it so well that when we beat this, everyone will want to do it just like we did" and "One day, all of this will just be a memory". Sometimes the days got so long and things got so bad that we'd say, "By this evening, this moment will just be a memory". There were times that she'd lie there sweating from the pain and look up at me with hollow black eyes and ask me to make her repeat those words after me. Those words carried us through some of the hardest times of Britney's life and I'm glad she doesn't have to live with those memories. "Just a memory" seemed so logical at the time, but looking back, I had no idea what I was saying.

Fourth grade was coming to an end and once again, Brit had missed more school than she had attended. And again, she had finished out the year on the honor roll and was ready to conquer fifth grade. Of course, we had to get through the summer and this one proved to be a challenge but, help was on its way and that help proved to be one of Britney's biggest blessings. She would be approved for a medically dependent children's program and with that program, came respite care. I had always had a hard time leaving Britney and, to be truthful, she was a lot to handle. This program not only offered respite care; they required it. I did get to act as a third party and hire someone I knew and trusted. I wanted someone who I knew was competent but also someone Brit would enjoy and be comfortable with. That person was Steph.

Chapter 9

When Stephanie came over, we played and played. I spent a lot of time in warm baths to keep my joints from hurting. She would make a wash cloth into puppets and sing opera. She would make the puppet propose to me and I'd dunk it in the water. We watched a lot of movies and my favorite was the Sound of Music except the romantic parts. I wanted to be just like Julie Andrews when I grew up. I could talk to Stephanie about anything but I didn't have to talk if I didn't want to.

—Britney

Fifth grade started off well. This would be the first year that Britney would be changing classes, and had multiple teachers, but most of her subjects were in her home-room. Brit's homeroom teacher was Miss Cara and she, like so many others, would become family. Miss Cara's extended family would become like our own and they introduced us to the world of barrel racing and play-days. Those wouldn't start until spring and we had a long, hard winter to get through first.

One bright spot in all of this was that we were told Britney had been elected to receive a wish from Make a Wish Foundation. The two ladies assigned to Britney started coming over, almost weekly, bringing gifts and waiting for Brit to decide what her wish might be. Her first wish was to meet Reba McEntire followed closely by Julie Andrews and Dick Van Dyke. Those were unusual wishes for a girl her age, and her representatives were thrilled, but because of our religion, meeting with a famous singer or actor was off the table. Finally, she decided she'd like to be a zoologist for the day and soon we were counting down the days and looking forward to a trip to San Diego. Brit would get a behind-the-scenes tour to the San Diego Safari Park, Zoo and Sea World and she was so excited.

She knew that she was going to get to go on a trip, she knew she was going to get to be a zoologist and she knew it was going to be really special but she didn't know when or exactly where she was going. I decided to throw a surprise party so that her friends and family could watch her be presented with her wish. To pull this off, I asked Ms. C if she could give Britney a ride out to my parent's house where a small group of people would be waiting, along with Make a Wish representatives, to surprise her. I asked Wings of Hope if they would want to join us and they brought two equine friends, Red and Phyllis. I had also asked Ms. C to spread the word to her teachers and tell them they were welcome so, on the day of the party, I shouldn't have been surprised by how many people showed up.

I knew Britney was loved, and I knew that she had touched the lives of so many, but seeing how many showed up really drove home how much she was truly cared for. Every teacher she had ever had, with the exception of a couple, showed up along with school staff, cafeteria ladies and even the superintendent. Plus, there were doctors and nurses and so many more. I had casually thrown out that we were going to do this but couldn't have imagined how many would set aside their plans and drive that far out all for the love of one little girl. There were so many people that Mr. Jay would have to take charge and announce when it was time to gather around. Mr. Jay was always there for any important event for Britney.

Brit was informed of the details of her Make a Wish trip and, a couple of months later, we left on the most organized and trouble-free vacation we've ever been on. Every detail was carefully planned out from our rental car, accommodations, special treats for the kids and the trip to the cockpit as we boarded the plane. Every extra was thought of including any kind of medical equipment or medical care, even numbers for the nearest on-call doctors. There's something about a Make a Wish trip that keeps your emotions on a roller coaster. It truly is magic.

You're blown over by others' generosity and the care and concern they have for your child but, on the other hand, you wouldn't be here if your child's life wasn't threatened. Behind every smiling picture is the thought of, *One day this may be all I have left.* Then the guilt hits, and you ask yourself, *Why am I thinking like that? Why can't I just live in the moment? I wonder what she's thinking,* and the one that I'm most famous for, *What if she's really not that sick and we shouldn't even be on a Make a Wish trip? What if the naysayers were right?*

As she got older Brit knew I doubted myself and, through her own observation, she knew why. It was she who reassured me on more than one occasion, she who pointed out the facts and she who reminded me that there were only a few of us living this and no one else mattered. Looking back, I pity the ones who stayed in the background, judging and spreading their gossip and opinions. Had they gotten to know Brit, not only would they have known the seriousness of her health issues, but they would have gotten to know her and the blessings that came with that.

As mentioned, I questioned myself repeatedly, every single day, and I was becoming known for asking those closest to our situation, "Is this all in my head or am I making her sick?" far too often. I don't know that, in her twenty years, I ever quit asking myself that question and frankly, I still do. I'm thankful for those who stepped right in, became part of Britney's world, supported me and constantly reassured me that I was doing all that I could. They filled in every gap, every need and every role that we needed filled and they were waiting to see and hear all about Brit's trip. They loved seeing the pictures and getting calls in the evening to hear about all she had gotten to do that day. Soon, the trip was coming to an end and I spent the last evening out on the balcony overlooking the ocean happy, but a little sad because. no matter how great, this wasn't a trip that was part of the life I had dreamed of. Nevertheless, we came home from that trip a little more relaxed, a little more rejuvenated and Brit more determined than ever to become a zoologist.

Once again, Brit's health started declining in the fall. She started up with her bouts of pneumonia but, where she had been battling dumping syndrome, now her body was doing just the opposite so the hospital stays and the dreaded NG tubes started up again. They were coming more often and each stay was lasting longer than the one before. Since Britney had an ileostomy, she shouldn't have been filling up with stool but her output had decreased significantly and the weekly KUB (abdominal x-ray) started again. Each one showed increased compaction and a distended colon. None of this made sense, and none of it should have been happening, but Brit never did anything by the book. Her doctors were stumped, I was stumped and she was paying a high price for us not being able to find a solution.

Watching your child choke on the stool that has backed up in her throat and seeing her retching to try to vomit it up, is gut- wrenching. Having to thread a narrow tube with a scoop on the end, up through her stoma (opening of her intestines), to dig out the poop that will eventually poison her system, was about all I could do in the moment. It was awful, but at least I was doing something to try to help her, and it was so much worse for her. I never lost sight of the fact that no matter how hard it was for me, I could not possibly imagine how hard it was for her. In between cleaning up the messes and trying to give her relief, I started searching and found two hospitals up north that seemed promising enough to offer us the little bit of hope we needed to keep pressing on. Looking back, that's what we always did when things got too tough to handle; we'd find that next strand of hope and grasp hold of it as tightly as we could.

I contacted Jan and she and Dr. Bryan started sending records and making phone calls to both hospitals. I called daily and soon we found out that our first choice had turned us down. At the time, I was disappointed and angry but looking back, I appreciate their honesty in letting us know they couldn't help. The other hospital said they would take Britney and the doctor who would be overseeing her called me himself to go over the plans and procedures for our upcoming visit. I was excited, and sure I had found the answer, so I shared my excitement with my husband and our kids. Despite the fact that it meant more testing and a lot of unknown for her, Brit was as hopeful as I was.

Zach was facing anywhere from ten days to nine weeks without seeing either of us but he took it all in stride just as he always did. Brit's dad started trying to work out the trip financially and was not excited or optimistic. I didn't understand why he couldn't get excited for this opportunity but in the end, he was right. This trip, the hospital and the leading doctor turned out to be a huge disappointment.

The stress of having a medically fragile child is always far outweighed by the blessing of him or her. Still, no matter how strong the bond or firm the commitment, the tension eventually catches up with us all. This trip would stretch us past our limits and set a precedent for the years to come.

Any time you have a set of parents who both want the best for their child, you can be sure they'll rarely agree. I saw it over years and years of hospital stays, in doctors' offices and while waiting surgical waiting rooms. Even in the best of circumstances, disagreements between couples are hard and unsettling yet you work through them to get to the other side. When you're living in hospitals with constant interruptions, no privacy and your sick child lying right there, everything gets shoved to the side and the tension just grows. Parents take turns, pull different shifts and only get a few minutes as they pass by each other walking in and out of their child's hospital room. We didn't even have that. I was Brit's only comfort and she begged me not to leave her even if her dad came to see her. Most stays, from the time we pulled into the ER to the time we were discharged, it was just she and I. When the stays stretched into weeks, their dad would come and bring Zach to visit. Nothing made Britney happier than seeing her brother and I could get a break knowing that I could leave her with him, and she'd be in good hands. I could go down to the cafeteria, gift shop or just outside for fresh air and I knew when I got back to the room she'd be okay. They were growing closer and closer and that was a big comfort to me because it often crossed my mind that if something happened to me, who would take care of Britney? Just as they were growing closer, their father and I were growing further and further apart. I can't blame this on Britney's health, even though it did exacerbate the situation, because the truth is we hadn't worked together from the beginning. So, the three of us heading north to an unknown hospital, an unknown doctor and in an unknown city didn't exactly promise a good trip no matter the reason. Mine and my husband's differences were completely set aside because medically, the trip turned into one of the biggest nightmares that Britney ever had to live through.

Jan, Dr. Bryan and I started planning with the doctors at this hospital in October. Twice, they switched the dates on us and we paid thousands of dollars to have our plane tickets rebooked. Plus, at the last minute, we learned that we would need to buy a portable oxygen condenser for Brit to fly with. Getting records from six of Brit's specialists and having them sent to six different specialists up north took up most of my days. Finding an affordable hotel room and a medical supply company near enough to deliver oxygen, and other supplies, proved to be challenging too. After weeks of planning on our part and theirs, we finally settled on an admission date in mid-February. There was daily communication and it seemed that things were set into place. If I could just get her there safely, it would be smooth sailing.

The plan was for us to fly in, drive to the hospital and meet with the cardiology team who agreed to wait for us even though it would be after hours. That part of plan went smoothly and Brit and I both found comfort in their competence and compassion. They ran tests and assured us they would look them over the next morning to see if she was stable enough to undergo anesthesia. When we finished that appointment we grabbed a bite to eat, found our hotel and settled into our new home away from home. Had I known what we would face the next day and for the remainder of our trip, I would have loaded her back up and carried her on my back all the way to Texas!

According to the schedule the hospital had provided, weeks in advance, we were to be admitted the next morning and she was to be seen by several different specialists throughout the day. As we were walking in the front door, a child coded right there next to us because the emergency room was right next to the main entrance of the hospital. This led to a discussion, with my ten-year-old daughter, where she asked what she needed to sign to make sure that what she had witnessed would never happen to her. She was adamant that she didn't want to be revived if her heart ever stopped. Britney had the intellect of a brilliant adult but, because of her illness, she looked about six years old. Having this discussion with my fifth-grade daughter as we waited to be admitted, was hard enough but looking at her and seeing a child so much younger, was surreal and unsettling for me. As it turns out, we had plenty of time to have this unpleasant conversation because we sat there for six very long hours.

Somehow, over the last four months of extensive planning and speaking directly to the hospital, not one person had any record of our carefully laid plans. They had no hospital room to put us in, no place for her on their crowded OR schedule and couldn't seem to find her extensive stack of records that not only had been faxed, but also mailed. Thankfully, I was well schooled in this lifestyle, and had run up against this incompetence before, so I had brought her records, printed out and labeled, so I could hand them over myself. After six long hours, their business day came to an end and we were sent back to our hotel room and told to show up in pre-op the next morning. Now, I would be taking my scared daughter straight into pre-op in a hospital she had never been in, handing her over to a doctor we had never laid eyes on and sending her back to an OR with a group of strangers. So we had no real plan for the next day, just to show up.

The next morning, we got up early and headed to the hospital with a very pensive and wary little girl. This was the first time her father had been to pre-op with us and he had never witnessed a scared, overstimulated Britney. I was used to working with a team that knew her, knew what worked for her and knew what didn't. While the nurses at this hospital were incredibly kind and understanding, whoever was in charge was one of those types who already had their mind made up and didn't want to hear any suggestions from the patient or the parents. I knew the drug Versed was supposed to calm the patient and make them forget anything unpleasant. I also knew that it had the complete opposite effect on Britney. She knew it too, but the doctor wouldn't hear it even after she had informed him, "Well, actually, Versed makes me go out of my head". So, they gave Britney the medicine, it didn't take long before it hit her and she became even more frantic and completely out of her head .

A typical child, at best, would be leery of a new hospital, new nurses, new doctor and all that comes with it. To put that on a child with

AS was overwhelming for her. Adding a medicine that she had adverse reactions to escalated the entire process. It also threw her off that her father was in the room and, although he had the right to be there, this was all new to him too and it just exacerbated the situation. The more upset Brit became, the more tense and angry her father became. When Brit screamed because she didn't want the IV, he got irritated with the nurses and, in turn, with me for holding her down and letting them put the IV in. In the few times he had ever dealt with her, his theory was to reason with her but, it never worked. With your typical child you can reason, promise rewards and generally talk them down. Those theories don't work with a child on the autism spectrum not to mention one who has been traumatized by all the things done to her in the past. Plus, by being in the hospital with us, in Brit's mind, he had trespassed into our world. I knew this but I knew to voice it would only make things worse. No matter how badly I wanted to make my point, or defend myself, I always had Britney's best interest first and foremost in mind.

I wasn't the most stable person in the room, but I was all she had, and I knew I had to stay calm. I was struggling because I was upset with the hospital, furious with the doctor, feeling a lot of unnecessary pressure from her father and, to be honest, I was scared. I had made what I thought were carefully laid plans. I had left my son for an unknown amount of time. I felt like if this didn't work, I'd never hear the end of it and I was beginning to think that any hope we had may have been false. Plus, as much of a privilege as it is to do whatever possible for our children, the fact is, the expense of a medically fragile child is astronomical. What if I had just wasted thousands of dollars? What if I was putting her through all of this for nothing and most importantly, what if it made things worse? Still, we had to try because what was our alternative?

All of this was running through my head as I lay beside her on that gurney, held her down and kept repeating, "It will be okay". She was so scared, she had stopped screaming and was staring me right in the eyes with a terrified look and saying, "Momma, please don't let them" until her voice gave out. Only I did let them do it. I lay beside her, in a sterile suit, in that horrible, outdated OR and still kept saying it would be okay.

It wasn't okay. It wasn't even remotely okay. In fact, I'm not sure that it was humane. The only thing I'm sure of is, that even truly believing it had to be done at the time, if I'd have known then what I know now, I would not have allowed it. Instead, she endured one of the most unimaginable situations she was ever put through during her entire twenty years of hospital life. It will never be lost on me that while she endured this, the one person she fully trusted and found the most comfort in held her down, whispered it would be okay and told her to try to quit screaming. I know Brit forgave me for that because that's the kind of person she was. She knew that we were both working for the same goal and we couldn't get there without what we naively assumed was the proper testing and help.

I'm not going to go into what went on in that OR except to say that, she wasn't asleep most of the time and even an adult, with the ability to comprehend the necessity of it all, would have felt violated. She was truly pushed past the threshold of terror before she was finally put to sleep and then, she woke up with all of the dreaded tubes that had been placed for motility testing. I had promised her this wouldn't be done, because I had been assured they would use the results from previous testing in Dallas, but like everything else we had been told, this was also untrue. Brit woke up in recovery still scared, gagging and feeling betrayed by the one person she trusted. Things seemed like they couldn't get any worse but, after hours in the recovery room, they did.

It was well after midnight when they finally found us a room but it would prove to be another slap in the face. On the website we had seen pictures of spacious, welcoming rooms but we soon found that there were no private rooms and they were small and outdated at best. Brit had no immune system, and these doctors had asked us to quarantine for two weeks before coming yet, they put her in a room with a two-year-old battling a nasty case of the flu.

I wanted to be relieved at finally being put in a room but, Britney would be waking up soon to a sick two-year-old wailing and coughing his lungs up less than four feet from her. I was worried about germs and I knew that would be the least of the other parents' worries when she became aware of all the noise coming from the other bed. As soon as I could find a nurse, I explained Brit's compromised immunity and tried to paint a picture of what it might look like when she woke up. The nurse was helpful but there were simply no more rooms.

Brit was starting to stir. I was getting desperate and would have taken a janitor's closet had it been offered. In Dallas, each floor had a treatment room used to keep scary procedures away from each child's personal room. These are always large rooms with plenty of space and anything you may have in a normal hospital room so with that in mind, I asked if there was one available. I was so relieved when the nurse said they were going to let us move into one but my relief was short-lived when I saw the tiny, windowless room we would be crammed into.

Still at least we were by ourselves, it was quiet and there was just enough room for me to wedge myself between the head of Britney's bed and the wall. That wall held me up while I held her head in place all night long to keep her from gagging and discourage her from pulling the tubes out. Sometime, in the early- morning hours, I dozed off and she did manage to pull several feet of tubing out of her nose. I knew that without this section of the probes, her motility testing would not be complete or accurate but by this point, I didn't care. I didn't let them put the tube back in and Brit got some relief from the gagging. Plus, I gained back some of her trust.

We still had to get through the motility testing and you can imagine the mess in that tiny, dark room so by the third morning, during shift change, when the new nurse walked through the door saying, "Is this *my* Britney from D8?" it was a welcome relief. By this point, Brit wasn't overly enthused but I was close to tears and so relieved to see a friendly, caring face. She was a traveling nurse and knew us from all of those stays in the hospital we couldn't wait to get back to. We finished out the testing, they pulled the tubes and we settled in for the night hoping for some answers the next morning.

Anytime a pediatric doctor, or really any doctor at all, has to deliver bad news it's got to be incredibly hard. We'd had our share of those conversations but with every one of them, I felt for the doctor. Those doctors had delivered the news in the most gentle, caring way possible and I knew it truly hurt them that they couldn't fix our girl. That wasn't the case with this doctor. This one, after squeezing himself into Britney's room, stood at the foot of her bed, looked at her and said, "There's nothing I can offer you. Take her home".

We were discharged pretty quickly after that and Britney was happy to get back to the hotel room. We went through our usual routine of scrubbing the hospital off of us. I settled her into her bed with some kind of craft and told her father I was going down to the lobby. I made it as far as the elevator before the tears and the vomit started coming. I sat on the floor behind a huge potted plant, puked into the roots and called a friend. I don't remember what all I said but I know that I asked her to let all of Brit's teachers know that we would be coming home with no answers and no plan for the future.

Brit took it all in stride and was just happy to be out of the hospital. We went to Target to buy some games, craft supplies and a basketball goal to hang on the back of the door because we had seven more days to fill; days we were supposed to be seeing other specialists and getting the help she so desperately needed. Instead, much to Britney's delight, we visited the aquarium and took a day trip a little farther north to see some of her father's family. She was thrilled to see all the animals and then spent time with family sledding in the snow but it was hard to be in the moment knowing that we were running out of time and had no real solution. As much as we enjoyed seeing family, I was so happy to board that plane and come home to Zachary, our community and our own doctors.

We came home disappointed but there was no time to sit, worry and stew about it. I had answers to find and I needed to do it soon. So, when Brit went back to school, I got busy researching and calling Jan. We were mentally and emotionally depleted, not to mention physically exhausted, but once again, one of Brit's teachers stepped up and wanted to do something to help ease her disappointment. Miss Cara asked us to follow her out to her parents' place where they had several horses. This brought a whole new element into Britney's world and through their generosity, she threw herself into barrel racing and play-days.

Looking back, Brit rode horses that were far too fast and far too much for her. But, as she said, "I'm dying anyway and I'd rather go on the back of a horse than laying in a hospital bed hooked up to a bunch of tubes". I know now that the risks of riding some of those horses, far outweighed the benefits but in one instance, a tumble off of one of those horses saved us from another hospital stay. Earlier in the day, an x-ray of Britney's abdomen had resulted in Dr. Bryan saying we needed to get back to the hospital for another dreaded clean-out. Brit hadn't had any output into her ostomy bag so we were not surprised but we were disappointed. Brit begged Dr. Bryan to let her barrel race that evening and head to the hospital the next morning and he relented.

Brit was on a horse that loved to fly and turn those barrels really tight. As they came around that third barrel the horse turned tight and Brit went flying, landing hard on her belly. The stands went quiet but she got up, led her horse to the alley, looked down under her shirt where she could see her bag and looked up grinning. "Well, actually, you can text Dr. Bryan and tell him we don't have to go back to the hospital. At the rate my bag is filling up, that fall just knocked the poo right out of me!" She was covered in dirt, grinning from ear to ear and that fall had indeed done its job and we didn't have to go to the hospital after all.

She spent every weekend that spring flying around barrels, poles and anywhere else she could on the back of their horses. Fifth grade was coming to an end and middle school was on the horizon but none of that concerned Brit but it did Ms. C; she was busy getting herself transferred to the middle school so she could continue to care for our girl.

Brit was busy winning ribbons, buckles and other prizes on the back of her horse. Between events, Mr. Doug would untack, feed and care for her horse while I accessed her port and hung IV fluids from the side of her horse trailer. Despite all of the little extras we had to haul along with us, this was one of Britney's happiest summers and she gained another bonus family in the horse community.

As if she wasn't getting enough time on horses, unbeknown to me, Brit had developed an interest in trick riding. One day, I got an email from Ginger Duke, a professional trick rider. Brit had used my email to reach out to her without telling me anything about it and Ginger not only wanted to let me know, she wanted to invite us out for the day. That day ended up being one of the most magical days of Britney's life. The first thing she did was jump on the back of a mustang, holding nothing but a rope around his neck, and flying around that arena. She learned some tricks and learned to Roman ride, standing with one foot on one horse and one foot on another. Not only did Brit learn new tricks that day, she made a life long friend, not just Ginger but of her family also. She also developed the love of mustangs that day and Ginger's mustangs would later become an inspiring part of Britney's story. Later, when Ginger had a horrific accident, it was Britney she thought about and who inspired her to keep going when she had to fight some of the same battles that Brit did.

We had a busy summer and anyone looking on would think that she was doing pretty well. The fact was that, not only did every play-day involve IV fluids and often oxygen, there were days of excruciating pain following every day in the saddle. Most times that Britney rode, during the course of the day, her hip would pop out of socket. She just kept riding and when the day was done, we would make a visit to my parents' where her Doc would pop it back into place. Most grown men would have screamed and never sat on a horse again, but not Brit. By the time the next Chisholm Challenge came around, she asked Doc if he could be available to come by and pop her hip in when it came out. He did; as she lay on the floor behind the seats in the arena, he'd pop it back in. The pain was worth it to her and pain had become such a part of her life that she could either give in to it, and not live, or she could bear it and live the life she loved. That life didn't just involve Chisholm Challenge and Wings of Hope; it involved another world of horses and equine events, a world that required a lot more involvement from her brother and myself. Britney had a way of expanding my world by forcing me into situations I would not have chosen for myself and this was one of them. I had no idea what kind of doors this new adventure would open for me.

While Zach had cultivated friendships through school, my friendships were still centered around the church. Entering into the world of play-days and horse activities, not to mention close bonds with Cara's family, pushed me out of my comfort zone and I had to start learning the ways of the world as I built friendships outside of the church. This complicated things. Not only were we participating in activities that would have been frowned on by the church if they had known, these people were becoming some of my dearest friends and part of Brit's biggest support system.

I never asked my kids not to tell what we were doing but we all knew that it wasn't something we could talk about at the church. We were breaking all kinds of rules. To name a few; Brit was wearing pants, we were surrounding ourselves with worldly people, there was dancing that we took part in at some of the banquets, there was alcohol served and, that's just naming a few of the sins we were participating in. Even though, by our church's standards, I knew that these sins would be on my head because, as a mom, I had led my children into this worldly environment, I wouldn't have had it any other way. Aside from school, this was one of my and my children's first real taste of the goodness, generosity and sincere care outside of our church walls.

For the most part, I was straddling a line with one foot in our church and one foot in the world. It wasn't hard because, as often as I saw the people from our church, I had no real relationship with them and our conversations were shallow and sporadic. It wasn't long before our parallel lives intersected and everyone became aware of Britney's other life and how much she was loved, admired and supported. She was loved for her spirit. She was admired for her tenacity, and strength in adversity but even more so, for her outstanding abilities as a horsewoman. She had a connection with horses that none of us will ever truly understand and she was supported.

Brit was so well supported that she earned the spot of the 2013 NARC & SP Queen for District Nine. Becoming queen was a great honor for Brit but with it came responsibilities one of which, was riding in the Fort Worth Stock Show and Rodeo Parade. This is where her worlds collided. Brit was riding one of Ginger's trick horses, sometimes sitting in the saddle and sometimes standing on top of it. She was quite the spectacle in all of her queen regalia and sequins, and there was no missing her when she rode by. In typical Brit fashion, she wasn't overly excited by all of the attention, but she didn't miss one detail, and as she rode through downtown Fort Worth, she spotted all along the route people from our church. Now it was out in the open and everyone knew that Britney was a rodeo queen. But, after everyone got through trying to condemn us, no one could argue with the fact that Britney was deeply loved. She was indeed deeply loved, cared for and cherished by the horse community, worldly or not.

I truly believe that God placed us in the horse community to be taught that people outside the walls of our church were truly loving, sincere and caring. I also know that on the day of Britney's big surgery,

Christmas Eve 2014, there was a nationwide prayer chain set up by the horse community through Cowboy Churches across the United States. Thousands of people were praying for Brit throughout the day. The horse community was not just a passing phase for Brit. They supported her and loved her to the very end.

Chapter 10

"Some people thought Ash was too fast for me but I knew he wouldn't let me get hurt. So, when whoever was at the gate, would say "are you sure you want to ride that horse" I would say, "I'm going to die any way and I'd rather die on a horse than in a hospital bed, connected to a bunch of tubes". They always looked shocked. Well actually, I guess they shouldn't have asked."

—Britney

The summer between fifth and sixth grade was a busy one. Not only did we need to get Britney prepared for the changes that would come with middle school, but her horse world was expanding and she was dividing her time between Wings of Hope and play-days on the weekends. WOH shuts down their classes during the hot summer, but Brit was still a frequent visitor, and after expending all her energy on the back of one horse on Saturdays, she would often spend several quiet days in the stall with Red. Both Brit and Red were slowing down, having less energy and happy to spend this time together.

Red was well past the age of any other horse most of us had ever heard of so it wasn't surprising to see him start to falter a little bit. It was assumed that he was just giving in to his old age. The vet had checked him many times and he was getting the best care along with the extra love and attention from everyone there. However, his patience seemed to be wearing thin with everyone except Brit. Each day as she arrived in the barn, his ears would perk up and he would nicker, something he rarely did. Red and Brit's bond became stronger and stronger during these quiet, long visits and one day, when she casually told Ms. Julie that Red had told her he was hurting, no one found that unusual. Instead, Ms. Julie asked her what she meant and she said that Red had told her his hip hurt and, even though he had given no indication of this, Julie listened. That week, Red was x-rayed and to no one's surprise, he had an abscess in his hip. Many times after that, Britney was invited to come ask their horses what was wrong and I can't think of a time that they didn't tell her exactly what they needed her to hear. Other horse people, who had heard of her gift, would invite her out to talk to their horses and as unreal as it sounds, I truly believe she did.

Red's abscess healed but he made it known that he wasn't interested in any interaction, other than with Brit and, being the good horse people they are, WOH decided it was time for him to retire. They asked Brit if she would like to take him home with her, and after asking Doc if we could keep him on his ranch, he came back to live the life he had been born into. His best horse friend, a crazy appaloosa came too, but that's a whole other story.

When a few of the instructors brought Red and Spud to their new home, we all felt that Brit and Red were nearing the end of their time on earth. Knowing that Brit was faltering as much as Red was, we all really believed that they would go together. Brit and Red spent the next couple of years riding and herding cattle all over my dad's property and, as Brit began to falter more, Red seemed to get stronger for her sake. She even took him to some play-days where she had every intention of keeping him slow and steady and just letting him have a good time. Many times, that forty-six-year old horse would come out of that gate like a stallion with Britney yelling, "Slow down! You're too old and you're gonna hurt yourself". She was laughing the entire time and so were the rest of us. It was a sight to see and Red was always rewarded with a bite of everyone's watermelon after each event. She never put a bit in his mouth and rarely put a lead rope on him. He would follow closely behind her to the concession stand, bathrooms and all around the arena like a faithful dog. Many times, I sat out in the blazing sun because that horse was napping under our canopy, often with Britney napping on his back. Red was Brit's best friend, soul mate and most trusted confidant and, those of us looking on, believe she was his. Had Brit been able to take him to middle school with her, the transition would have been easier on her. As it turned out, it wasn't much of a transition because she was getting sicker and rarely made it to class.

The switch to middle school was made easier on both of us because, once again, Ms. C changed schools with her and someone new entered Britney's life. Mrs. Brady was Ms. C's aide and before long she had won Britney over and was spoiling her just as much as Ms. C had always done. Middle school can be a big challenge when it comes to being a homebound student. You're suddenly trying to get work from six different teachers and your only communication is through email. Mrs. Brady had a knack for getting anything Brit needed and Brit was quite sure that Mrs. Brady could run the entire district. I am still sure of that. It wasn't long before Mrs. Brady had earned a permanent place in Brit's heart. Mrs. Brady and Ms. C were some of the last few Brit spoke to before she slipped into a coma years later.

Even though she rarely made it to class, Brit had decided she wanted to be part of the percussion section in the band. As always, the school and teachers supported her decision and never made her feel ostracized for rarely being there. Her band teacher sent home a small xylophone and Brit proceeded to not only teach herself to play it but to go on to earn a first division at the school's area competition. On the few days she made it to band class, one of the boys took notice of her and worked up the courage to ask her out. He was a sweet boy, and later made a fine young man, but Brit being Brit, responded to his question by saying, "Drop dead"! They stayed friends all through high school and Brit is one of the few who can honestly say that a state senator's son asked her out and she told him to drop dead. When I asked her why, she shrugged and said, "Well, actually, it was just the first thing that came to my mind".

Once again it was Fall, and Britney started declining along with spending more and more time in the hospital. If she wasn't fighting dumping syndrome, she was severely constipated. If she wasn't dehydrated, she was holding on to too much fluid. If her lungs were working right, her heart wasn't and vice versa. Her teachers were supportive, Brit kept up with her work and her grades were all high. Basically, it was just a repeat of all the years before and when the school year came to an end, Brit had only made four full days of her sixth-grade year. Though her attendance was low, her grades were anything but, and she was academically ready to move on to seventh grade.

Sixth grade had come to a close but the summer wasn't looking too promising. In the past years, Brit had improved in the late spring but not this year. Despite adding calories and eating huge amounts, she was drastically losing weight and losing it at an alarming rate. With the dehydration and weight loss, along with blood work, it was determined that Britney was not absorbing nutrients so basically, no matter how much she ate, she was starving. She was getting thinner and thinner, her hair was falling out and her teeth and nails were starting to streak, a sure sign of malnutrition. As a rule, I have always said never Google your symptoms but it's hard to look at your child and see their sunken cheeks and hollowed eyes. It seemed like all of her energy had been sucked right out of her. I had tried everything I could get my hands on from appetite stimulants to all-natural remedies, expert dietitians and more but nothing was working. She was emaciated and every morning the scales went lower. It seemed like every option had been exhausted so I broke my own rules and went to the internet.

I found that, in other countries, they were giving kids with cystic fibrosis of the gut, breast milk. Brit didn't have CF but what if this was the answer? And, how was I going to get my hands on it? I knew there were mothers' milk banks but I assumed that they would be highly unlikely to give milk to a teenager whose mom just had a hunch. As I saw it, I only had one choice. That was to try to produce the milk myself and that was the next thing I researched. First, I wanted to make sure that it couldn't harm Britney in any way and that would require a call to Dr. Bryan.

Dr. Bryan was like part of our family, but he was also very proper, and I had a lot of respect for him. I had run a lot of hare brained ideas by him over the past several years but this one was on a whole new level. This idea was one that neither of us ever openly discussed. Instead, I called Jan and ran this unconventional idea by her. Then, it was her job to run it by Dr. Bryan. I never heard what was said during that discussion but it was decided that, while we didn't know if it would help, it certainly couldn't hurt.

Next, I had to go tell my husband that his thirty-nine-year old wife needed to order a hospital-grade breast pump because she had decided that she was going to keep their fourteen-year- old alive by producing her own breast milk. He was about as comfortable with that conversation as Dr. Bryan would have been but he ordered the pump and never said a word. He also never said a word when I started rapidly gaining weight, began having night sweats and eventually developed mastitis.

I did everything in my power to boost my production. I drank non-alcoholic beer and consumed huge amounts of brewer's yeast. Our whole family was unknowingly eating lactation cookies and I was having appointments with a very squeaky pump, every two hours, around the clock. That is how I started. Every two hours, for twenty minutes night and day. I had not breast fed a baby in thirteen years, but I was determined, and before long my efforts paid off. I'll never forget how Britney responded when I told her what I had done and asked her if she was willing to drink it. I was bending over her, changing her ostomy bag and not ready for the fountain that shot out when she started laughing. She laughed and laughed and said, "I can have so much fun with this". "Can you imagine people's faces when I tell them that you are breast feeding me?"

That is where I drew the line and let her know that we wouldn't be telling anybody but her doctors and she would be drinking it out of a cup. Everyone was pleasantly surprised when Brit put on forty-nine pounds and grew six inches over the next year. We still faced a lot of hurdles during that year but at least she wasn't starving anymore and she had the energy to fight all that was about to be thrown at her.

Chapter 11

Eating and drinking anything made me feel horrible, it hurt my stomach and made me feel nauseous. I would have been embarrassed if anyone had found out what I was drinking but my mom put the milk in PediaSure bottles with Ovaltine in it so it looked like chocolate milk. It tasted sweet like chocolate milk too. I started to grow again and I had more energy. I didn't mind drinking the milk but hated the reason I had to drink it.

Zach made me laugh a lot. He either made me laugh or he was incredibly annoying. He was one of the only people who could make me smile. He, and Reba McEntire, I always watched Reba and laughed.

—Britney

Unlike other years, where things had started off okay and then gone downhill, this year started off badly. It was good to see that she had grown and filled out but her pain was increasing and nothing seemed to help. She had pain management, and they were great, but even they couldn't put a stop to whatever we were dealing with. And that was the thing, none of us knew exactly what was going on. Some of her doctors were truly concerned not only for her health, but for her mental well-being because they could see the level of pain she was having. Several of them had a history with Britney; they knew how tough she was and knew that she was not a complainer. However, some of these doctors were new to her. Not only were they new, but they were less than compassionate, arrogant and not willing to budge from their assumed diagnosis.

Dr. Bryan, along with her other established doctors, was doing all he could for her and trying to communicate with the new doctors but nothing was getting done. She spent weeks on end lying in the hospital drugged and miserable, and for the first time, we started losing all hope. The only thing that kept us going were the nurses who were just as frustrated as we were. Those nurses became our lifeline, constant support, friends, therapists and ultimately, family. They supported my advocating, Brit's frustrations, shared our fears and helped with any farfetched solutions I came up with including the breastmilk.

They could have acted like I was insane, and I'm sure there were some mutterings in the nurses' station, because I would have been muttering too. Here was this thirty-nine-year old mom with her fourteen-year old 5'4" daughter lying in the bed while she was over in the corner pumping. It would have been easy to look the other way or even make it hard on us but they didn't. Instead, they hung a Breastfeeding Mother sign beside the door, moved us to a larger room with the space for me to pump, asked often if I was getting enough to eat, stored my breastmilk in the refrigerator and even offered a discrete, friendly Moooo as I walked past their station. They truly went above and beyond and Brit and I never looked back on that time without remembering their kindness, compassion and generosity.

Still, no matter how hard the nurses were trying, we couldn't seem to get the floor doctors on board and after weeks turned to months, we opted to go home. It was scary, and Brit was on some strong narcotics, but coming home put the doctors who knew her best in charge of her care. More importantly, going home had the added benefit of being able to visit Red.

By now it was bitter cold, unusually cold for Texas, and a trip out to see Red was going to be hard on Britney. But, it had been weeks since he had been brought to the hospital to see her and it was worth the pain, and any other misery she had to go through, to see her old man. I piled blankets and pillows in the back of our SUV, snuggled Brit in and drove out to the pasture. Red knew the minute we came through that gate and he came running and vocalizing his excitement. We stopped at the barn, got a bucket of feed and pulled right in the middle of the pasture. I can still see Britney lying in the back of the car, barely able to lift her head, but holding the bucket of feed while her toothless old man ate his dinner. When he was done, he gently put his head into the car and laid it on her legs. They stayed that way for over an hour while she slept and he drooled leftover feed all over the blankets. The next morning, we had to return to the hospital.

We were there for over a week but it was apparent that nothing was going to be done this time either. Finally, one of the specialists said there was a medicine we could try but, because it wasn't approved for children under eighteen, we would have to try it at home and not in the hospital. Once again, we returned home much sicker than when we had been admitted but at least we could try a new medicine in hopes that it would work. The new medicine did not work at all, but now, Dr. Bryan had enough cause to ask for a surgery consult and to order it STAT.

Dr. T, the surgeon who took our case, was a breath of fresh air. He had the typical arrogance that comes with every surgeon but he also had a kindness and humor that put us quickly at ease. He ordered imaging and we went downstairs to get it done right away. Before we had made it home, he called and said if I could get Britney in to see Dr. Bryan the following day and he would clear her for surgery, he would put her on the schedule.

The appointment the following day with Dr. Bryan is one that I will never forget. Brit was barely conscious. She was yellow, waxy and covered in a blistery rash. The room was quiet as he, Brit, Jan and I sat there because, really, there wasn't anything to say. He went about his business of listening to Brit's heart and lungs and doing all the things he was supposed to do but we all knew he was just going through the motions. Months later I found out that he and Jan were thinking exactly as I was, that this would be her last visit to his office. Before we left there, both doctors had spoken on the phone and Brit would be going into surgery early the next morning, Christmas Eve 2014.

All night that night, I spent most of the hours standing over Britney's bed watching her sleep, listening to the oxygen condenser and watching her chest to see if she was breathing. When I wasn't standing over her, I was sitting in the living room praying that going through with this surgery was the right decision. The surgeon had been brutally honest with me and I knew there was a chance that Brit wouldn't come out of this alive but we also knew that if we didn't go through with it, we wouldn't have her much longer. Before daylight, I woke Britney. She slipped on her zebra print robe, along with her cowboy boots, and we headed to the hospital.

We were the only ones in admitting and we were the first ones in pre-op that morning. When you've spent so many hours in the halls of hospitals, you learn to read the doctors' and nurses' mannerisms, smiles, meaningful looks, pats on the back and other subtle signs. It was very quiet in our room and very somber. We did all try to be cheerful for Britney's sake but she was so sick that she just lay there silent and listless. This was another children's hospital that was well acquainted with Brit and I'll always be grateful that they let me scrub in, walk to the OR with her and hold her as the anesthesia took hold and she drifted off to sleep. During all of this, Brit remained quiet until right before she was asked to take a deep breath from the mask over her face. She knew the drill, and she knew what they were going to ask of her, but she lay there silently. As the anesthesiologist asked her to take that deep breath, she looked right at me and asked, "Momma, am I going to die?" I bent over, kissed her cheek and told her no but the truth was, I wasn't sure.

Shortly after, Brit's body went limp and that's always been my cue to leave the room. I remember walking through the double doors and nurses were lined up telling me how brave I was, offering a comforting hug and telling me how they had offered up prayers for our girl. I remember trying to get out of that hallway to get back to the waiting room feeling like I was suffocating and trying to peel that sterile bunny suit off. As I came around the corner, there were my parents, Brit's dad and our friends Bob and Vicki. The six of us sat there for the next nine hours going through my mom's ample supply of snacks, magazines and Diet Dr Peppers.

Parents were coming and going all day. They would come to the waiting room, wait a short while and then their child would be ready to be taken home. As the late-afternoon hours came around, everyone was gone and there was just the six of us left. Finally, a nurse came out and asked us to step into a side room as the doctor would be meeting with us soon. It felt like an eternity before Dr. T walked through the door and slumped into a chair. He sat there silently for what was just a few seconds but seemed like hours before he looked up and said, "You're one lucky momma... no, you're one *blessed* momma!"

He had just stood for hours over our daughter literally untangling her intestines, separating some organs from others, repairing eleven bowel hernias and getting rid of that ileostomy bag. He was exhausted, sweaty and wearing her blood but he looked like an angel to me and he stayed well into the night to keep an eye on our Britney. I was so relieved, and I was beyond exhausted, but full of adrenaline at the same time. That was a good thing because we were entering into one of the longest waiting games of our life.

When Britney and I had finally gotten to her room, everyone else went home. Shortly after, my best friend, Sheila, walked in the door with her pillow, suitcase and open arms. She had driven all the way from Oklahoma and she stayed there with us for the next five days. Those were five very long days but, we still had a lot of days to go. In the past, our biggest obstacle after surgery, was Brit waking up from the anesthesia but this time, she wouldn't rouse at all. The nurses and I would do all we could to stimulate her, and try to get a response, but we got nothing; not even a wince, much less a kick or a punch like we were accustomed to.

On the fifth day, Sheila left in the afternoon to head home and I settled in for a quiet evening. There was still no response from Brit. I was still pumping and the nurses were still storing it for when she could eat again. Brit was getting her nutrition through her veins, her port was accessed, she had an IV in each arm, a nasal cannula for oxygen and a tube down one nostril into her stomach to suction any fluid that was building up. Around 1:00 a.m., monitors started beeping and Brit's coloring got really bad. I ran out of the room and there was a doctor coming out of a patient's room next door. He could tell something was wrong and ran in as our nighttime nurse raced in and, suddenly, things got really hectic. Soon we were headed to ICU with the doctor running beside the bed and a nurse on the bed starting yet another IV in Britney's leg. For the next couple of hours, Brit was on one side of the curtain with a medical team while a chaplain stood quietly with me on the other side. She finally stabilized but was too critical to be moved to one of the ICU's more private rooms. I sat in a chair beside her, with a nurse close by, for the rest of the night. The hospital had been generous enough to let us keep our room upstairs so that I could go up and pump every four hours, take a shower or change clothes. That was our routine for the next several days until she improved a little more, roused a little more and was able to move back upstairs.

We were there for another three weeks, and during those weeks, a lot happened. Brit's incision, through no fault of the hospital or the surgeon, became infected and had to be opened up bedside. That resulted in a wound vac, along with wound care for the next nine weeks. On top of the bulky wound vac and excruciating pain, Brit had to learn to have a bowel movement in the toilet for the first time ever. She was too weak to make it to the bathroom and her doctors decided it best for her not to sit. She knelt beside her bed and had to try to go in a diaper. It had to have been degrading but she never complained; she just apologized for me having to clean it up. No amount of me telling her what a privilege it was to be there beside her stopped the apologizing. Later on, Brit liked nothing better than the shock value of telling everyone that, "Well, actually, I was still drinking breast milk and got potty trained when I was fourteen years old". She got the biggest kick out of that but rarely bothered to explain the circumstances behind it.

It was almost February when we finally went home. She was still connected to the wound vac but had no need for oxygen or IV fluids through her port and she had the prettiest pink cheeks we had ever seen. Brit left the hospital in the same cowboy boots and zebra robe she had arrived in and we headed straight to the barn. She was in so much pain from the car ride that she was retching but she still wanted to pay a visit to her best friend. He was so happy to see her but seemed to understand that he needed to be gentle and to be careful where he nuzzled her.

Brit missed riding in Chisholm Challenge that year, and she missed riding in the parade, but she still had something to look forward to. Ginger Duke had decided to compete in the Mustang Magic competition and she had decided to name her mare Britney's Inspiration. For the Mustang Magic competition, each competitor selects a wild mustang and has approximately 120 days to train it before the three-day competition. On the last day of competition, the trainer gets to put on a freestyle performance of their choice to showcase what they have taught their mustang. Ginger asked if she could tell Brit's story through different obstacles and tricks that she had taught Britney's Inspiration to do.

The evening of the final performance, Brit and I drove to Fort Worth to watch Ginger perform. Britney had a bulky wound vac holding her belly together and she was in excruciating pain but she wasn't going to miss that performance for anything. We were seated behind the judges and watched Ginger take Britney's Inspiration through each step starting with the one labeled "They said I wouldn't make it". The next steps were labeled "Pain", "Suffering", "Obstacles" and so on. At the end, Ginger stood on her horse and, as Britney's Inspiration flew around the arena, Ginger held a flag that said, "But I did!"

We sat through the other trainers' performances and, as the judges tallied up the scores, a lady approached Britney and asked her if she would like to present Ginger with her first-place prize. Two ring stewards carried Brit down the steps into the arena and, with that bulky wound vac hanging from her shoulder and all that tubing circling her belly, she was honored to hand Ginger Duke her first-place ribbon. Before Brit hugged Ginger, she did exactly what I knew she would do. She put a hand on each side of Britney's Inspiration's face and they shared a moment first. Britney praised that mare and all of us looking on were sure that we saw the mare nod before she turned to the cameras.

For six weeks, after she was discharged, we made the trip to Fort Worth, Monday through Friday, for wound care. It was painful and exhausting for Brit but we stopped to see Red on our way home and he seemed to know when she started to get her strength back. He was always gentle but he would demand a little more attention and a little more movement from her each time she visited. Brit was doing so well when she went back to see her surgeon that he lifted one restriction early. He let her climb back on Red's back as long as she promised to be careful. Her version of careful was to ride in the next play-day with a back brace across her belly for added support and protection. This time, it was me yelling "Slow down! You're going to hurt yourself!" but she was laughing and I trusted Red to know what was best for her.

By the time Brit was released to go back to school, the year was coming to an end and in April, we got the best news ever. Britney was in remission. We still had to work with physical therapy. Plus, it took a while to get her stamina back so she missed most of her eighth-grade school year too. Once again, after attending only eleven full days of middle school, she was in the top of her class and inducted into the National Junior Honor Society.

Now we had to get ready for the big transition into high school, but Brit was once again in for a surprise. Ms. C and Mrs. Brady were magically transferred to the high school right in time for Britney's freshman year. Brit wasn't really surprised; she knew they wouldn't let her go alone, but I was so relieved and the three of us started coming up with a plan to make this change as easy as possible for Brit.

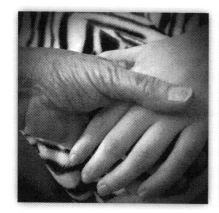
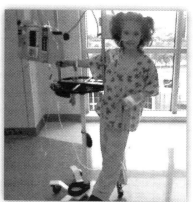

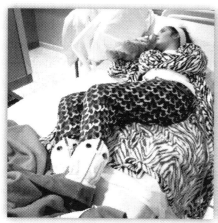
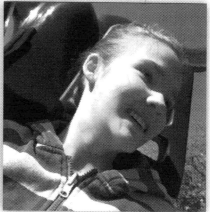

Chapter 12

*"I don't know why anybody was surprised. I
knew Ms. C and Mrs. Brady weren't going to
let me go over there by myself. Ms. C doesn't
trust anyone else to take care of me and Mrs.
Brady doesn't trust anyone else to spoil me
just right. Plus, they like to see what Mom
packs for me to eat at lunch and me and Mrs.
Brady liked to talk about Harry Potter".*
—*Britney*

The first day of high school came and Brit headed for a new campus
riding with Cat and Ms. C. I didn't worry and it didn't upset me that
I wasn't dropping her off for her first day because, by now, it was only
right that she start this new chapter with Ms. C. Plus, I had no doubt
that Mrs. Brady already had everything in order and had preplanned
for any possible upset. *Mrs. Brady always has a plan!*

Two weeks before school started, Ms. C and I sat down with
Britney's teachers and explained her health situation. She was doing
well; we were hopeful and we weren't planning on anything happening
but we felt we should prepare them just in case. One thing Britney
had signed up for was the school's FFA program and this was the best
decision she could have made.

We were thrust into the FFA way of life. The land of predawn
mornings, frequent meals from Whataburger, sketchy hotels, grand

prix driving and anything else beyond my comfort zone. At the same time, I got to know some of the most well- behaved, hard-working kids, attend some of the most rewarding competitions and tag along with some of the best, most dedicated teachers I've ever known. I didn't know how well I would be received as I tagged along behind my high school daughter to every competition and on every overnight trip. I tried my best to stay in the background and give her the independence she so deserved but still, Brit's mom was always there. This would have bothered me in high school but not Brit and soon, after I started showing up with homemade cookies, it didn't bother any of the other kids either. I would follow the bus and then, when we arrived at our destination, I would stay in my car only getting out to use the restroom.

On competition days, it's not unusual to leave the school at five in the morning and not return until nine or ten at night. That makes for a really long day but I was determined to let her have as normal of an experience as possible. For the first few months this worked out but then, Brit joined the Vet Tech team. They won many local competitions and soon we headed out on our first overnight trip.

Mr. Willson was the perfect coach for the team of four girls and they loved and respected him but, what man wants to be in charge of four teenage girls? I know that me tagging along did him a favor with Britney's care and it helped that I was there for the other girls also. Having to accommodate an adult female, that he didn't know very well, had to have been an added inconvenience but he didn't show it.

I had this on my mind as we headed out on that first trip and I felt a little bit unsure of my role in his routine. When we stopped to eat, there were several choices of eating establishments. We selected a restaurant and, while Mr. Willson and I were placing our order, we realized that all four girls had abandoned us to eat at another restaurant next door. What could have turned into an uncomfortable dinner became the defining point of our relationship over the next four years. We acknowledged that this was definitely different, but we both wanted the best for Brit, and we developed a good system as we traveled over Britney's high school years. Mr. Willson was one of Brit's favorite teachers and probably the one she was most comfortable with, although she felt that way about all three of her FFA teachers. He was also the one responsible for hauling those girls all around Aggieland, during a state competition, and doing his best to woo Britney into bleeding maroon. Five years later, he stood at the end of her funeral and softly called the Muster before the Aggie Fight Song was played for her recessional.

The truth is, when Britney signed up for FFA at the end of her eight-grade year I was less than excited, a little leery and way out of my comfort zone. But, just as she had done so many times before, she brought us into a new world that made me a better person. It opened up new experiences and brought some of the most valued friendships into my life. Brit truly loved every part of FFA and she loved every person in her FFA family. I will forever be grateful to that honorable and character-building organization.

I'm thankful she joined and thankful she got to participate as much as she did because she was only a few weeks into the school year when her health started failing again. I had noticed that Britney's appetite had slowed way down and noticed that she would start to eat something, take a couple of bites and say she was full. I could tell she was hiding something but I didn't know if something was going on at school or something was wrong at home. Then, Ms. C noticed that she wasn't eating at school either so I had to sit Britney down and ask her if her stomach was hurting her again. She shook her head no but she wouldn't look at me. Then, her eyes filled with tears and I knew she couldn't hold out on me. "Momma, it's happening again".

That's when the tears really came. She had been hurting for weeks but didn't want to tell me and she didn't even want to admit it to herself. Even though she was said to be in remission we still didn't fully know what she was in remission from. Though we celebrated, it was always in the back of our minds that it would likely rear its ugly head again. I called Dr. Bryan. He sent us for a KUB and, as soon as I saw it, I knew things weren't working right again. Brit refused to look at it because she knew it would confirm what she suspected. The results threw us back into the vicious cycle of flushes, enemas, clean outs, hospital stays and finally, the dreaded NG tube. Along with all of this came tests and procedures, more rounds of anesthesia, more prodding and poking and this time something was added to Britney's plate. This time she had to deal with PTSD on top of everything else.

She was being treated at two different children's hospitals in the D/FW area and there had been scary, unsure times at both. For one small surgery we found ourselves back in the same pre-op room and taken into the same OR that Brit had had her big surgery in. She was shaking, but held it together, and once again I was standing over her in the OR as the anesthesiologist told her to take a deep breath. Brit said, "Hold on." The doctor removed the mask and Brit looked right at me and said, "Momma, am I going to die?" I understood her fear and reassured her that this was nothing like the last time and she was going to be just fine. So, she looked up at the doctor and said, "Dr. A, last time, y'all told me I wasn't going to die but y'all really didn't know. I had a big chance of dying and ya'll weren't honest, so please tell me, am I going to die?" Dr. A was emotional as she took the time to explain to Britney that this wasn't a big surgery. She was going to take care of her and she wasn't going to let her die.

No matter what was tried, how many nights we spent in the hospital or how many different medicines they added to Brit's regimen, nothing worked. Despite the fact that the pain was getting worse and worse, not to mention that Brit's spirits were plummeting, no one seemed to have an answer. After a while, it felt like we were in the same predicament we had been in several years before. Brit couldn't sleep because the pain was so bad and I couldn't sleep because I couldn't do anything for her. One night, I got on my laptop and started searching for anything I could find on pediatric gastroenterology. That's when I found Cincinnati Children's Hospital, the top pediatric gastroenterology program in the United States. I set my alarm for seven the next morning and sent a joint text to Dr. Bryan, Jan and Dr. S, Brit's GI doctor we had been so lucky to have for the last ten years. We all went to work and, while we were still sitting in the hospital, records were being sent, phone calls were being made and tests were being done so that the results could be sent to Cincinnati ahead of us.

After receiving all of Brit's records and test results, the panel of GI doctors at Cincinnati Children's Hospital agreed to take Britney's case. If I could get her there and with the understanding that they couldn't give me any guarantees, they would see what they could do for us. They couldn't tell us if we'd be there three days, three weeks or three months.

They couldn't even promise that she would be coming back home alive. They only promised that they would try their best to find some answers.

By now, Brit was back on TPN, total parenteral nutrition, and had a PICC line in her arm. Her port had been taken out because we hadn't used it in so long. With a PICC line in place, it allowed me to mix and run her TPN over eighteen hours each day instead of having to have a nurse do it. Packing up all of the sterile supplies for the line, the bags of TPN and the vials that had to be added to it proved to be a challenge. However we traveled, we were going to be hauling an awful lot of stuff. At home, this was well organized in four plastic storage drawers and the TPN took up most of the refrigerator. We knew that we had to travel with at least five days' worth of her nutrition and it all had to be kept at a certain temperature. We needed to be able to make it through five days because, in order to get TPN in Cincinnati, Brit had to be enrolled in their home health system.

We were discharged from the local hospital with a week's worth of TPN, multiple vials of vitamins and medicines that had to be added to it, two tandem IV pumps and a host of other medical supplies. Our hotel was booked and the hospital was waiting for us. One of my friends, a retired nurse, graciously agreed to ride up to Ohio with Britney and me and then fly back home. Our entire car was packed full and very little of that was personal belongings. We pulled out in the evening not knowing how long we would be gone, what we would be facing when we got there or how in the world we were going to pay for it all. Thankfully, Brit knew nothing of the financial worries; her plate was full enough just trying to hang on until we could get there. I stopped around midnight at a seedy, unlit gas station on the border of Texas and Arkansas where I filled syringes, mixed TPN and set IV pumps all in the glow of a cellphone flashlight.

I was beyond grateful for our friend Robbie for traveling with us. Not only was she a constant source of entertainment for Brit, but she was a calming force for me. Robbie and I had spent many late nights and into the wee hours of the morning talking, or messaging, trying to find the next step in Britney's care. Had it not been for Robbie's experience and Google search expertise, I wouldn't have come up with half of the ideas I did. Plus, Robbie was a strong woman, someone you wanted in your corner and she brought a sense of comfort and safety for Brit and me. We were used to traveling into different cities at all hours of the night, just the two of us, but we were traveling to a whole other world compared to our small town. It was so good to have someone there with us.

Eighteen hours after leaving Texas, we pulled into a rest stop somewhere in Kentucky, unhooked the TPN and threw all the used supplies in the trash. The trash can was immediately swarmed and some frightening-looking characters started picking apart the soiled tubing and pulling at the used bags in search of the needles they hoped to find. This was our first reality check but it didn't hold a candle to what we witnessed in Cincinnati. It was a world away from our quiet little hometown but a world we would make our home in for nine weeks and, though it was a scary world compared to what we were accustomed to, it was the best decision we could have made.

Unlike the trip we had made up north to a different hospital, Cincinnati Children's (CCH) ran like clockwork so when we pulled into our hotel that evening, we had already received a phone call confirming our appointment early the next morning. Brit knew that this appointment would start with the dreaded NG tube but she knew that she badly needed help and this was probably our last chance to get it. Our morning started at six with me having to insert a suppository and Brit enduring the cramping leading up to being cleaned out. Then, we made the trip for our eight o'clock appointment and, even though the hospital was less than six miles from us, we had to allow forty-five minutes to get there. Cincinnati traffic is like nothing I had ever driven in and I had driven during rush hour in LA. It was raining, the wind was blowing, Brit was in pain and no matter how brave she was trying to be, her PTSD was getting the best of her.

CCH is an international hospital and it's not different from an international airport when it comes to parking, security and all the different cultures mixed into it. As busy as it is, and as huge as it is, it's also very warm and welcoming to every patient of every culture. If you're at CCH, you are very sick or, at best, have a complicated diagnosis and that goes for meeting the criteria of their Ronald McDonald House too.

Stepping into this world comes with many different emotions. First and foremost, the relief and appreciation of being in a hospital as highly regarded as CCH and the hope that comes with that. Then, you see how sick all the children are around you, reality sets in and you can't deny how sick your child is too. The worry in other parents' faces reflects your own and gives voice to all the feelings you've been trying to keep tucked away inside. As much as we parents are seeing and feeling this, we know that our children have to be feeling it that much more. It's a scary feeling mixed with sadness but, something about being surrounded by other children and parents who are walking the same path you are, brings you comfort. There's a solidarity that I imagine is a lot like a brotherhood that soldiers share. We are all fighting the same battle, in trying to keep our children alive, and doing our best to stay strong for them.

I think even Brit somehow felt that she was less alone there and when we got off the elevator and stepped onto the GI floor, as scared as she was, she knew we were where we needed to be. There were two nurses and their care and compassion showed through the minute they introduced themselves. They acknowledged how unpleasant this procedure was going to be and promised to do all they could to make it as painless and as easy as possible.

For the first part of the test, Brit had to lie on her side and have a catheter, with a balloon, inserted into her rectum. Although there were tears pouring down her face from the discomfort, along with the bad memories of previous hospital testing, she lay still like a trooper. Through her tears, she kept apologizing and assuring both nurses that they weren't hurting her and her tears were no fault of theirs. They, in turn, kept reassuring Brit that her tears were nothing to be ashamed of and they understood how scared she was and all she had been through during her short life. They did their best to ensure her dignity and talk her through every step of the way. They did win her over but the next step was to place the NG tube and as hard as she tried, she couldn't hold it together.

The nurses stepped out of the room to give me the opportunity to try to calm Brit and help her to gain some control. She was frantic and screaming but not in a combative way; she was screaming out of pure terror. I tried soothing her and pulled all the tricks out of my bag but nothing was working. I'd like to be able to say that I stayed calm and understanding but I had to take the upper hand, be the mom and get stern. I climbed on the bed behind her, wrapped my arms around the upper half of her body and my legs around the lower half, lowered my voice and reminded her that this was likely our last chance. We had driven over a thousand miles to get help and it was up to her whether we went through with it or went home. For the first time ever, I hinted at what could happen if we didn't get her the help she needed and she, being miles ahead of me, knew exactly what I meant. She quieted down and leaned her head back against my shoulder. The nurses came in, and as Brit shook violently but didn't fight them, they inserted the NG tube.

I can't dwell on the times that I had to get stern with her or the guilt consumes me. I know I didn't have a choice. I know *she* didn't have a choice. I know we were both working toward the same goal but that doesn't make it any easier. She endured more in her lifetime than most of us could ever imagine.

As promised, before we headed back to the hotel they removed the NG tube and we went for a nice dinner. The next morning, we headed to the hospital for a long, but less invasive, test. The nurses had done such a good job of winning Britney over the day before that she decided she could do some of this by herself. That was the kind of trust CCH built with Britney and in the years following, they never lost any of the ground they had gained with her. That afternoon, we met Brit's new doctor, in person, for the first time and he also made a friend of Brit. Once again, things ran right on schedule and he had all of her test results and a plan of treatment to go along with them. The downside of this was that Brit would have to endure another round of motility testing but the test itself had advanced and would only take two days this time.

On the morning that Britney was scheduled to be admitted to the hospital, it was cold and rainy and we were rushed to grab our bags and make it to the car because the fire alarms were sounding in our hotel. Everyone else was running down the stairs empty-handed but we had some of our bags and Brit couldn't move very fast because she was so weak. As all the other guests gathered in the appointed spot, Brit and I loaded into our car and headed to the hospital not knowing if the rest of our belongings were going to be burned up in a fire or not.

After being admitted and being shown to our room, the clean out began and it lasted all day and into the night. At five the next morning, we were wheeled down to pre-op and Brit was prepped to go into the OR. Everyone was so kind and truly wanted to make it the best experience they could to try to help her past some of her bad memories. Even the anesthesiologist, upon hearing of Britney's love of animals, traded cases with someone who could discuss animals on the same level that Brit could. Everyone in that hospital went above and beyond to make us feel at home but still, when I walked out of the OR, leaving my baby girl on that table, I felt helpless and afraid. As I sat there, a thousand miles from home, I tried to calm myself but that was hard to do.

I tried standing at the windows but it was barely light outside and it was pouring rain. I tried reading magazines but couldn't concentrate on the words in front of me. I tried playing on my phone, scrolling through social media and anything else that I could think of. I wanted to call someone just to hear a voice but at home, it was two hours earlier and everyone was sleeping. It was only a few hours before the doctor came out to talk to me but it seemed like it was all day. He had found a few problems, had fixed them and then inserted all the tubes and attached all the probes in preparation for the motility testing to be done the next day. Knowing that Brit would be coming out of anesthesia gagging and choking on all the tubes, they had agreed to let her sleep most of the day and wake her up that evening. I should have slept while she was, but I was too uptight and that day seemed like it would never end. Only the night proved to be even longer. By now, we had it down to an art and I took up my position at the head of Brit's bed to help hold her in place in hopes of alleviating the choking and gagging.

Early the next morning the machines were wheeled in and the motility testing was started but at least this time, it would be over in one day. I think knowing that it wouldn't be dragged out over several days helped Brit get through it but when it was completed, and all the tubes were removed, she asked me to promise her that she would never have to do it again. I had let Britney have control over her medical decisions very early on. She knew that she always had the option to say that enough was enough and, she knew I would support her. I still made her that promise. I promised her that she would never have to have motility testing ever again.

We were discharged from the hospital but still had weeks of outpatient appointments scheduled with all different specialties, including a genetic specialist. Genetic testing had come a long way since Brit's first round of testing and we would have the results back within a week. Already the GI department had come through for us and fixed several of Brit's issues and now, she was in the hands of one of the top rheumatologists in the world. Dr. G had retired from the National Institute of Health and CCH was lucky to have him. We were beyond blessed to be put into his competent hands and to not only benefit from his knowledge but from the knowledge of his colleagues all over the world. After years of suspecting that Brit had been misdiagnosed, through no fault of her doctors, I was looking forward to getting some real answers and hopefully some direction in which way we should go from here. With the progression of genetic testing over the last ten years, we would have a much better map to follow in hopes of finding a true diagnosis.

We both showed up to that appointment with high hopes but didn't dare say it out loud. I remember Dr. G sitting down with his thick stack of results and Brit hanging on every word. I'm glad she did because somebody needed to come back home and explain it to her doctors here and that wasn't going to be me because I didn't understand a word of it. She did, and I could tell by her expression that she was relieved to finally have some answers. But then again, maybe she was just glad to finally talk to someone as smart as she was. If she were here, she could write another book and explain it all but she's not, so I'll give it my best shot.

Brit was misdiagnosed ten years before this. Genetic testing was not what it is now and, working with the limited markers they had, her doctors had made an educated diagnosis. Now, sitting with pages and pages of data, we still didn't have a firm diagnosis but we did know that Britney had some irregular chromosomes. We didn't have any real answers, and that was disappointing, but I left that appointment unbelievably relieved.

After sixteen years of blaming myself, thinking I had passed defective genes on to my daughter, it was proven that this had not come from me at all. That was a burden that I hadn't realized the weight of until it was lifted off of my shoulders. That was a weight that I desperately needed lifted because all of the years of watching her go through the suffering that she had, and watching most of it alone, was taking its toll on me. Brit and I had always been in this together, just us. Some of that couldn't be helped, but some of it could have been, and the lack of support through this entire journey was wearing me down.

Dr. G asked to have her DNA, along with extra blood samples, sent to the National Institute of Health. Although we were disappointed to not get a firm diagnosis, we still felt hopeful that at least he was going to continue to try to get us some answers. We never did get those answers but her DNA is still at the NIH and still being tested for research purposes in hopes of helping others.

We still had six more weeks of appointments and testing scheduled and thankfully, I got the call from Ronald McDonald House saying they had a room available for us. Brit and I packed up our hotel room, contacted our home health nurse to let her know we were getting a new address and drove to our new residence. I'm not a crier, never have been, but when we pulled through those gates and walked in to be welcomed by a volunteer, I fell apart. Brit got to rest in another room but I had a stack of paperwork to fill out and an orientation video to get through. I bawled through the entire thing. I know it was just relief for Brit and me to be somewhere safe and to have other families around us that were walking the same path we were.

It continued to rain every day, it was dark and gloomy and the days were getting colder and shorter but not in that safe haven of the RM House. It was warm, bright, friendly and every need was graciously met. Being in such a safe place meant that I had more time to myself because I could leave Britney in our room happily doing her schoolwork or reading. She had brought her school laptop and had no intention of falling behind on her studies. She rarely left our room except to go to appointments or visit therapy dogs brought in by volunteers. She was still weak and tired, but the pain was gone, and sitting in our room day after day suited her very well. I, on the other hand, literally thought I was going to lose my mind from loneliness and fear. I could be all bright and cheerful in front of Britney but as soon as I got a minute to myself, there was a lump in my throat, a heaviness in my chest and I could barely swallow liquid much less anything solid.

To be clear, I'm beyond grateful for CCH and RM House, and I know that Britney was too, but those weeks were some of the hardest and loneliest of my life. We did have visitors, and they are truly what held us together, but still, when I look back on that time, I get a pit in my stomach and a feeling that can only be rivaled by the last few weeks before losing her.

Finally, we had our last appointment, our last test was completed and it was time to go home. There was ice on the car and snow on the ground when we left what had been home for the past six weeks. We headed to the airport to pick up a friend who had thankfully flown in to accompany us on our trip back home. We decided to give Brit full control of our trip and spent the next five days hitting every drive-through zoo and wildlife park from Ohio to Texas. Pulling into our hometown, and into our driveway, was bittersweet. It was so good to be home and even better that we came home with answers and solutions for Brit's issues but, on the flip side to that, what if something went wrong? We were about a thousand miles from CCH and the thought of having to turn around and go back any time soon was overwhelming.

Two days later, we were sitting at my parents Thanksgiving table and we were all getting an immense amount of joy out of watching Britney eat. She ate her weight in ham, mashed potatoes, sweet potatoes, salad, rolls and a big piece of pumpkin pie. It was a good time, made even more special because we had spent so few out of the hospital, but still, that nagging feeling of *what if* was never far from my mind.

I wish I had lived in the moment but to be fair, any of us with medically complex children know that the tables can turn on a dime. We get so used to expecting the unexpected that we can't just relax and live in the present. For me, it was very important to stay a step ahead of whatever curveball we were thrown next and, though that kept me prepared, it robbed me of a lot of joy. I could see on Brit's face that she was still skittish too. Any time her stomach felt off she would get that pensive, apprehensive look and quit eating. We both had to learn to live the normal that others take for granted and are accustomed to but we were beyond grateful for the reprieve.

After Christmas break, Brit went back to school and was able to pick back up where she left off not just academically, but she was also competing in FFA competitions. As the year came to an end, she ran for a spot on her chapter's officer team and won. She held the position from that year until she graduated. When school let out for the summer, we were in a good place and we finally started to breathe a little easier and enjoy each day.

Chapter 13

I don't know why people worry about taking their SAT'S, it wasn't hard at all. I'll tell ya this, some of those boys haven't grown up at all this summer and I don't know why they're bothering to test, no college is going to want them. Of course they won't act any different in college and they'll come home with their tales between their legs. Some of them are actually smart they just don't know how to act.

—Britney

Brit's sophomore year in high school started off pretty well. She still had her moments, and there were days I had to threaten her to get her through the front door, but overall she was functioning like a normal high school girl and the other students rarely saw her act out. Actually, it didn't matter if they did because they all knew her, respected her, admired her for her strength and truly loved and cared for her. The other kids were aware that Brit had some extra needs and were willing to offer a helping hand, but they also treated her as their equal. Brit truly couldn't have been placed in a better school district when it came to her teachers and peers.

When we had been in Cincinnati, Ms. C had called because the student council wanted to do a fundraiser for Brit. We had never accepted funds, or tried to raise any ourselves, because there were always those less fortunate than we were, and we didn't feel right taking money that others could use more. Ms. C explained that everyone knew that but the students really wanted to do this to show Britney just how much they cared. We discussed it and decided that we would accept their offer but set the funds aside to help others. That's something that Britney always wanted to do but we never had the extra money to give.

STING week is a five-day fundraiser led by the student council, that the students hold each year for a classmate with challenging circumstances. The kids in our district, from kindergarten through twelfth grade, donate and hold an assortment of competitions to raise money. There had been two previous STING weeks but this year, before the designated week even kicked off, the entire community got involved. It seemed like everywhere we went there were donation buckets along with services and items being auctioned off to raise money. Then the actual STING week commenced and the games began.

Each day, the students could buy a ticket that would get them admitted to the gym to watch the games. Brit was into the *Hunger Games,* at the time, so this was the theme of the competition. Kids volunteered to participate in relay games that ranged from talent and speed to slipping and sliding through mayonnaise, mustard, ketchup and there was even some squid tossing. Coaches and teachers let the student council shave their beards, color their hair and wax their legs all for a price that had to be bid on. Brit's FFA teacher and fellow Aggie, Mr. Willson, wore a Texas Longhorn shirt for an entire day. There was also a talent show and after-school activities including different sports events, a dodgeball knockout and a concert with some well-known performers. There was also an evening of attractions, food trucks and Zachary getting his ears pierced on stage in front of the community. Fast-food chains held fundraising nights and local shops contributed with free products and labor. The student body accomplished all they had set out to do, plus much more, in showing Britney how much she was loved and cared for.

On the final day, the entire student body gathered in the gym for one last game and for the big reveal of the total amount raised. Brit had won the area vet tech competition two weeks before, so she was competing at the state level down at Texas A&M when a teacher sent me the video of the reveal. Brit's fellow students, teachers and our community had raised well over $20,000. That total hasn't been matched since. While we were thankful for the funds, the love and care shown to our girl far exceeded any dollar amount.

By now we were living out from under the shadow of her GI issues but her heart and lungs were acting up more and more. On the days Britney was able to attend the games in her honor, she did so in a wheelchair. That is how she attended all school functions from that day forward. I didn't see it then, but looking back, she was growing weaker and weaker and the only time she wasn't in that chair was at home or places that she didn't have to walk much.

At some point, I realized that although she was free from her GI issues, she really was getting sicker and if she was going to live her hopes and dreams, I was going to have to completely devote my time and energy to her. With Zach grown up and independent, this made my decision a little easier. Brit had her sights on "Aggieland", and if she was going to live her dreams, I was going to live them too. We still had two years of high school left but if she was going to get to go, I knew I had to commit or tell her that it wouldn't be possible. I decided to commit, completely.

I remember walking in our room to tell her father what I had decided. Anytime Britney had talked about Texas A&M, he hadn't said a word and I wanted to make sure he was on board. I didn't want Brit to get her hopes up, make plans, put herself through the stress of trying to get accepted and then when she did, for him to tell her she wasn't going. We had left the religion we had been in but it was still very much ingrained in me to submit to my husband. I wanted he and I to agree in supporting Britney and her plans for her future. I already knew that, together or not, I was going to support her and I was going to make it happen for her no matter what. For the first time ever, I didn't ask about planning. I just said that we were going forward with our plans. I remember saying, "I need to know where you are on this because she is already working on getting everything in order. It's going to take everything in her to have the strength to do this and I'm not going to let her put in all the work, achieve her goal and then have you pull the rug out from under her. She is *going* to go. I need to know if you're going to support her or if I need to start asking for help because there are too many people who want to help her to succeed and they will make it happen."

I knew her father would do whatever he could, for Brit's sake, and I knew that asking him to support not only her but me moving two hours away was a lot. He finally ended up relenting and supporting her wishes but the contention between us got even more tangible. Had we still been a part of that church, I would've had to give in and do the *perceived* biblical thing. Later, I would have regretted killing Britney's hopes and dreams and would have known that there was nothing biblical about my decision. I would have lived with that guilt for the rest of my life, and Brit would have been robbed of the experience ahead of her, not to mention those who would have been robbed of the gift of knowing her and the brilliance she had to offer.

When you make a right decision, other people's thoughts and opinions don't count. You can be certain you've made the right decision when there are no regrets. To me, the decision was clear. Brit couldn't go to college without me and she had come way too far, and had way too much to offer, for me to give up on her now.

Did I want to move two hours away where I didn't know anyone? No! Did I want to be surrounded by a bunch of kids on campus day after day? Not at all. Did I know I was going to be lonely? Yes, but I couldn't have imagined how lonely it was really going to be. I could barely stand the thought of leaving Zachary, my family, my friends and all that was familiar but, I had two years to prepare for all of that.

For now, Brit's body may have been slowing down but her social life was getting busier, thanks to her FFA family. She was competing, and making a name for herself, and she had built strong friendships with the girls on her team; three of them, were going off to college sooner than Brit and going to be Aggies. She continued to be a part of all things Ag but her days on campus were getting fewer and further between and her homebound teacher was coming more frequently.

Every day was a roller coaster when it came to blood pressure, heart rate, fluid retention, kidney function and so many other things but because she wasn't in pain, we still thought we were in the clear. We were still making monthly doctors' appointments but there was no real treatment, just monitoring. That's the way it was going to have to be if Brit was going to be able to live her life the way she wanted to. I started focusing on ways to give her more independence and her biggest key to independence came by accident later that summer.

Brit finished out the school year and we knew it was going to be a quiet summer because she wasn't moving much at all and we were going to spend two weeks making a trip to CCH for her checkup. One day, she was lying in her bed and I asked her what she thought might help to lift her spirits. She said she wanted something small, an animal that she could just hold, something that would always be there, just for her. She decided to start looking at rescue sites in hopes of adopting a dog. My stipulations were, if I was going to have to put up with a dog in my house, it needed to have short hair, no shedding and no scragglylooking hair. It couldn't be hyper, badly behaved or yap all the time. She started looking online, and I started making calls, but trying to find a smaller breed dog that fit my criteria seemed pretty impossible. When one shelter said they had exactly what we were looking for, warning bells should have gone off and I should have known that they weren't listening to my description but, we went anyway. When we were taken back to the kennels, we were introduced to a soaking wet, scragglyhaired dog and Brit was in love. Zach was laughing because he knew this dog didn't fit my description at all but I was watching that dog and the only one more in love than Brit, was him.

Needless to say, Puppy slept in Brit's bed that night and every night after that at home, in hospitals, in surgery centers and in hotels as he accompanied her to every FFA competition she attended from that day forward. He was beside her at her graduation and in pre-op and post-op. He oversaw every IV and blood draw and he stayed the duration of hospital admissions that lasted weeks on end. He also learned to love Red, just as much as Brit did, and I will always believe that Red knew she would be in good hands when it came time for him to cross that rainbow bridge. Brit and Puppy finished out her tenth-grade year together, he traveled two thousand miles to CCH and back with us that summer and then it was time to get him certified so she could start her junior year with him by her side.

Chapter 13

"Hey Mr. Willson, I'm going to be an Aggie! I was still in high school but I had been accepted into Texas A&M and that's all I could think about. I knew it was going to be hard well, the getting around would be but I was pretty sure I could handle the classes. I had to get ready for graduation and I had to get Mr. C and Mrs. Brady prepared for me to graduate. They couldn't go off to college with me but I thought they might try."

—Britney

Britney's junior year of high school started off uneventful. She was raising a lamb to show for FFA and was competing in the Ag Business contest. She was signed up for dual credit classes and inducted into the National Honor Society. Life was as good as it could be and things seemed to be normal, inasmuch as it could be with all of the daily ins and outs of Brit's health issues.

Over all, that year was one of the smoothest she had in all of her school years. If it hadn't been for the fatigue and overall maintenance of her health, she would have been in school most of the time. She did have one surgery that kept her from showing her lamb but other than that, there were no hospital stays and no emergency trips to Cincinnati. We did head to CCH that summer for her routine checkup where her doctors were so happy to see her progress. Then it was time for her senior year.

This last year of high school proved to be much like her earlier years. It started off smoothly but with fall came a decline. There were no real GI issues but her heart and lungs just wouldn't cooperate and she was struggling. Most hospital visits were so that she could be "tanked up" meaning, she would get the fluids and any other support she needed to get her back on track. Even after these visits, and with her excitement over the possibility of going to Texas A&M, I could see a change in Britney's demeanor. Where she had been relatively carefree for the last nine months, she was starting to show a weariness, a slowing down and even a bit of resignation when it came to her health issues.

Through all of this, whether she was at home in her bed, admitted to the hospital or recovering from one of her multiple set backs, Brit kept studying and kept her grades up. She also started applying to colleges, applying for scholarships and taking classes to better prepare her for taking her SATs. She didn't give up, no matter how bad she was feeling or how much pain she was in; she kept her eyes on her goal and Puppy stayed faithfully by her side. Puppy had taken over as her main cheerleader since Red had crossed the rainbow bridge and, as much as Red was missed, the timing was right because Brit soon found out that she was going to Texas A&M and it would have been too difficult to take Red with her.

First, we had to get through graduation. Ms. C and I had spent many long nights wondering if we would get Britney to the next grade. When we had to have those tough discussions, we would always finish them up by saying, "Just think what it will be like to watch her walk across that stage". Most of these times, we were highly doubtful that we would be able to see that day take place but, here we were. Early in the year, I had asked the superintendent if it would be possible for Ms. C to present Britney with her diploma as she walked across the stage. He agreed and we managed to keep it a secret until a few short days before the ceremony when we had to order Ms. C's stole to wear with her cap and gown.

Britney had never willingly hugged anyone, ever! Of course she had been hugged by others, but she never liked it and never wanted it. She knew that it was socially acceptable but with autism, touching and interacting was not something she needed or wanted. Ms. C had always wanted a hug from Britney but knew it would probably never happen. As graduation grew near, Britney was bothered because she really wanted to hug Ms. C. when she handed her her diploma. She asked me what she could do, not just to get her comfortable with giving Ms. C a hug, but actually show her how to physically do it right. We decided to hang my robe on the doorframe of her room and as she would pass by, she would hug the robe to get herself acclimated to actually giving a hug. When graduation finally came and Ms. C stood on the stage to give Britney her diploma, Britney walked up that ramp, took her diploma and gave Ms. C the best hug that she could. There were tears from all, especially Ms. C.

Despite the fact that Britney was beyond exhausted, there was a graduation party going on at our house. Of course we didn't invite a whole lot of people, but the people who had made so much of an impact in Britney's life were on hand to cheer for our girl in her own home. This was not just a graduation; this was a girl who had been fighting for knowledge and for just being alive her entire life. At least she proved to herself that she could achieve anything she wanted to in the academic world of public high school. As everyone congratulated Brit for her amazing accomplishments, she was holding it together and thanking everyone for coming. As soon as Dr. Bryan told Brit how proud of her he was, he walked over to her father and said, "You must be Britney's father. I know you are proud of her." Then Dr. Bryan came over to me and said, "Look what you did! Look at all of those cords of honor!" I reminded him that, without his support and guidance, Brit likely wouldn't have been here to celebrate. We were both quite emotional, both of us knowing that without God, she surely wouldn't have been here at all. Britney was worn out and soon went to bed. Most people left but Mr. and Ms. C, Mrs. Mc, Mr. and Mrs. Brady settled in to have a couple of celebratory drinks in honor of our brilliant girl and all of her accomplishments.

The following week after graduation, we were off to New Student Conference at Texas A&M. It was at this time I realized that not only was this going to be hard on Britney, but it just might kill me. Maneuvering a wheelchair over 50,000 acres and miles and miles of walking is a feat that's hard for even a fit college student. My preconceived notion that I could do whatever it took as long as I put my mind to it, was put to the test before we even made it to the first location we were supposed to be at. I had always been a runner and in pretty good shape for my age of right over forty. My concern was not only to make it to our destination but to not let Britney see that I was struggling so hard. This was a Texas summer day and the temperature was high, with the heat index of 114 degrees, and the humidity level was as miserable as the temperature. I tried to keep my breathing even but it finally came to gasping and wondering if I was even going to make it. The last thing I wanted was to make Britney think that she was being a burden to me. She was so grateful for everything I was doing and she told me repeatedly. That truly kept me going and gave me strength for another day.

Chapter 14

I don't want to be the sick kid. I want to try to walk to class like all the other students. We can leave extra early so we can walk slow and take breaks. I'm not nervous, just ready and I hope that I actually learn something.

—Britney

We had the summer to get prepared to move to College Station, Texas. When most kids head off to college, they spend their summers shopping for their dorms, figuring out transportation, meeting their dorm mates and all of the things that go along with starting college life. For us, the summer meant preparing to move into her college apartment, getting enough medical supplies to stock up for the semester, finding a company to provide her oxygen, IV pumps and so on. Plus, we were trying to find a hospital that would work with her doctors here and prepare for all emergencies. We also had checkups with each specialist and any other medical professionals who were part of her team. Besides all of this, I had to sit down with Dr. Bryan and we had to come up with a plan on how to triage any difficulty that came up. We had to decide on a protocol that we could follow. I would have to determine whether it was safer to get her to a closer hospital, with all new doctors, or put her in the car and make the three-hour drive to Fort Worth. There, at least she could be treated by her own team. The more we tried to prepare, the more I realized how unprepared I was.

That realization brought two things into perspective. First, we were going to be winging it, and though her doctors were only a phone call away, it would still take hours to get to them. Second, I was going to be completely on my own. There would be no Ms. C down the street, no Jan who could come running if we needed her and no familiar nurses right around the corner if we had a problem we couldn't solve. It suddenly hit me that it was just going to be Brit and I in that town, far from home and facing it all on our own. Only Brit's excitement kept me focused and quieted my doubts.

Before we knew it, we were settled in our apartment and preparing for the first day of college. Even though this is what we had worked for and dreamed of, it was surreal. I was forty-four years old, living in a college town, having to use my navigation to get anywhere, trying to find our way around a campus that was bigger than our hometown and realizing I had just left my friends and family behind. Britney, on the other hand, was more determined than ever, more excited than I had ever seen her and completely at home because she had me and Puppy and we were her world. That in itself made it all worth it to me.

It was the first day of classes and Brit had decided that she was going to walk, not use oxygen and start off college as a normal student, not the "sick kid". She saw it as a fresh beginning, where no one knew her, and she could invent a whole new life. I fully supported that and we decided that on the first day, I would wear a backpack and follow behind her a ways to see if she had the stamina to make it to each building. There were so many students continuing their education that I just looked like one of them being that many of them were my age and older. We had worked her schedule to where she had two classes back to back and then a two-and-a-half-hour break to go back to the apartment, use oxygen, get IV fluids as needed and get a nap in.

I would have her lunch ready and she would eat it in the car on the way back to campus. Then she would complete two more classes, have an hour in the library and then head to her last class of the day. That was three days a week. On the other two days she had a morning class, a three-hour break and then returned for a three-hour lab followed by an hour long group-study session. That's what our schedule for the first semester. We would get through the week, load the car up and head home for the weekend.

As I mentioned, Britney wanted to start her college years as just a regular student, and not the sick kid, and she did. The first day, she made it the whole day walking to each class with Puppy right on her heels. She was exhausted to the point of stumbling and weaving but she kept walking and was determined to do it the next day also. It was sweltering and the humidity made it feel even more hot and stifling than it already was. Brit had been using oxygen if she walked any significant distance and relied on her wheelchair just to make it from the car into her doctor's offices. Now, she was walking farther than she had in years in the punishing heat and, most of the time, walking uphill. She was living her dream and she was determined to do it on her terms and the way she so deserved to.

On the second day, I was keeping my distance behind her and it was evident she was struggling. Against my better judgment, but just as hopeful as she was, I didn't step in. I just let her be. We hadn't walked far when her knees buckled, she went down, Puppy took his guard over her and several students stopped to try to help. When I got to her, she was white as a sheet, clammy and her pulse was thready. I had asked two male students to help me carry her over to the shade so when she came to, it was just us. After the confusion wore off, she fought tears and said, "I guess I'm going to have to do this in my chair". She had a look of defeat but, by the time I went to the car and brought her wheelchair back, her resolve had returned and we went on to class.

That incident summed up Britney's college career. We would hit a snag, figure it out and go on to class. By the second week, Brit's determination and lack of self-pity had already been noted by her professors and fellow students. Once again, her peers stepped up and started looking out for her; only at A&M, Brit wasn't the sick kid. Here she was the brilliant kid, the one others went to for help, the one everybody wanted as their lab partner and the one that piqued her professors' interest. They not only wanted her to succeed; they knew she would succeed and they wanted to be part of her story. They weren't just impressed with her grades and her performance in class. Her drive, fortitude and humility were not only noticed but remembered later by all who had been inspired by her.

Soon the first semester was over, finals were all done and we got to head home for several weeks. I loved being home where I could see my friends and family but besides catching up with Zachary, Ms. C and Mrs. Brady, Brit was bored stiff. She saw no need for a break between semesters and had me take her to the used bookstore so she could stock up on used text-books to study on her own. By now, she had decided to give up her coveted zoology degree for something "a little more challenging" that could "actually teach me something". She settled on a degree in astrobiology. That degree consists of astrophysics, planetary science, biology and physics. She was thrilled. I was thrilled for her but wondered how I was going to get clearance at NASA where she would have to do her last two years of training before earning her doctorate.

We were home, I was socializing and Brit was studying and happy to be in her room with her books and spirals full of her meticulously recorded information. Things were good and the breath I'd been holding for eighteen years was slowly being released. We had made it; we were at college and living some semblance of normalcy. Then on Christmas Day, Brit's body threw us yet another curve-ball, the one we would fight till the very end.

Chapter 15

"Munchausen By Proxy, really??? First of all, I can't have Munchausen by Proxy. I would have to have Munchausen Syndrome, you would have to have Munchausen by Proxy but, do they really think I'm that ignorant? More than that, do they think I'm naive enough to let you get by with that? I wish they would have questioned me as in depth as they questioned you. I would have told them how inept that doctor was. It was an insult that she didn't think I could list my diagnosis, history and symptoms in proper medical terms instead of just saying my tummy hurts or I can't potty or my heart is broken. First of all, I'm in college. Second of all, I've been living with this for 20 years. Most importantly, I'm way smarter than the doctor and seem to know more about testing, meds and protocols."
—Britney

Christmas Day was a good day and we had gone to spend time with extended family. Brit was happy as she worked a jigsaw puzzle with her aunts and played games with her cousins. She was relaxed and laughing and Puppy slept down at her feet. Puppy gave the first alert that something wasn't right and when I looked at Brit, she had lost all color in her face and had gone quiet. When I asked her what was wrong, she said she suddenly had a stabbing pain in her ear. By the time we got home, she had a raging fever and was retching from the vertigo. It was a sleepless night and I texted Dr. Bryan at eight o'clock the next morning.

Knowing Britney's history with ear infections, he went ahead and called in antibiotics in several forms to try to attack it from every angle. Still, by Monday, she couldn't wake up and I had to have help getting her into the car so we could head to see Dr. Bryan. When we got there, she still wouldn't wake up and he did his exam in the parking lot and I'll never forget how frustrated he was. He wanted the best for his girl and he knew her well enough to know that this couldn't be a simple ear infection.

After some hydration and new meds, we were able to get her to wake up but the rest of her Christmas break was spent visiting one specialist after another trying to get some answers. Every time we got in the car, every time she had to walk and every time she moved her head, the pain would increase and she would start retching. The retching would increase the pressure, the pressure would magnify the pain and the pain would cause the retching to get worse. It was a vicious cycle. Britney's motility was compromised, and she couldn't vomit because her esophagus had very little movement, so she just dry heaved instead. It was a constant circle and I can only imagine the thoughts going through her head as she pushed herself through each appointment only to be disappointed with no answers.

Eventually, we were referred to Dr. Marc and Britney instantly trusted him. He was as brilliant as she was but he didn't give her any false expectations. He had done testing, and he knew what we were dealing with, but because we never knew how Britney's body would react, we knew any treatment would be an experiment. Dr. Marc promised that, no matter how long it took or how frustrating it became, he wouldn't give up on her. He promised to stick with her and keep trying everything possible and, he kept that promise.

No matter what medicine we tried or which procedure was done, Brit's body wouldn't respond the way it should and soon what started as a common ear infection, developed into random brain abscesses.

They would develop with no warning and never in the same area of her brain. Soon it was time for her second semester to start and we left for College Station with no answers. She was still as sick, still in as much pain, still dealing with the vertigo but more determined than ever to go to class. And, she did.

She went to class dealing with all that she had going on and her grades didn't slip but, her body did. Infections and doctors' appointments, along with home medications, turned into ER visits. Then before long, we were spending two to three weeks at a time in the hospital. We would come home to be admitted to the hospital she was most familiar with and whose doctors were most familiar with her.

Britney had been to many pediatric hospitals but the two closest to us were her primary hospitals. Brit had grown up riding her IV pole down the halls, playing in the playrooms and making a family of all the staff from doctors to janitors. She loved everyone but had formed a special bond with many nurses and I had become close friends with several of them. As much as we hated a trip to the ER, surgeries or long-term admissions, they made it much more bearable. Usually, by the time we had to go to the hospital, things were bad enough that we breathed a sigh of relief as we pulled in the parking garage.

By now Brit was nineteen, past the age that a pediatric hospital would service, but because of her rare condition and her doctors being so familiar with her, she was allowed to stay on as a patient. Britney considered these her hospitals; places that brought her a sense of peace, comfort and, at least in the past, some solutions to her pain or whatever issue was plaguing her at the time.

I felt the same but, being the mom of a medically fragile child, I knew from other parents' experiences that I was always being watched as closely as Britney. As worrisome as this was, in a way, this brought me a sense of safety because no one questioned my decisions more than I did. It brought me comfort to know that the best decisions were being made for Britney despite any opinion I might have.

As a second semester of college started, Brit began having more and more symptoms, more trips back to town for doctors' appointments, more need for IV fluids and meds and soon she needed more hospital stays. We were making two and three trips a week between College

Station and the DFW area, sometimes making the trip in one day so she didn't miss a lab or another important class. None of Brit's professors required this of her, and several encouraged her to take care of herself and make up the classes later, but no matter how miserable she was, she kept going. Six different times we scheduled a procedure on a Friday so she could be back in the classroom on Monday. Many of these procedures were to clean out abscesses in her brain and some involved cutting out small parts of her skull in order to reach the affected area.

Because her doctors supported her drive to be involved in the classroom, they allowed us to do IV antibiotics and hydration at home. By now I could start an IV, but I wasn't especially good at it, and I dreaded it even more than Brit did. Our nurses were at home in the DFW area and College Station was 181 miles away. One of her nurses would start her IV on Sunday and we'd head to College Station with the IV bag hanging from the car visor. I'd keep it running through the night, pull it the next morning and we would head to class. Often we'd repeat the process midway through the week and it was becoming more and more evident that Brit was not absorbing fluids like she should and was going to have to rely on IV hydration. IV fluids, and keeping her hydrated, were the only way to keep her heart rate steady and her blood pressure regulated. We'd been down this road years before; only she had a port and it was much easier for me to poke a needle through her skin and hit that port than it was for me to try to hit a vein.

Brit's veins were also showing signs of being stressed and worn out. Because she couldn't absorb fluids orally, it didn't matter how much water she drank or how much salt she consumed; she couldn't stay hydrated which kept her veins hidden and inaccessible. When the nurse could manage to access one, it was after thirty minutes of heat from a heating pad, a lot of thumping the area where the vein was and many unsuccessful pokes. When she finally got in, through no fault of her own, the vein would blow resulting in six or seven more attempts. Brit's arms looked like a battle-ground and her resolve was starting to wear thin.

In the early spring, we found ourselves admitted for another brain abscess. We'd only been out of the hospital for two weeks, following another ten day admission for another infection.

Brit couldn't sleep, not just from the pain but from the retching and vertigo. No tubes this time, no major surgeries but just as miserable as in the past; only now, she had Puppy to comfort her. He only left her side to go for a quick walk and to potty. The nurses took turns giving him treats of peanut butter they had brought him from downstairs.

Brit was taken into the OR to have the abscess cleaned out but other than that, it was just lie there and wait for the meds to work. When she could stand it, Brit studied and later took two finals on her laptop as she lay in her hospital bed. It wasn't required of her and her professors had reached out, through email, to make sure she knew she had the option to make up any test later. She was determined to take them on time, was determined to score toward the top of the class, and she did. She scored in the top percent lying in her hospital bed, miserable and overcoming her seventh bout of sepsis.

During that hospital visit, Brit was seen by most of her specialists and those who weren't directly involved with this admission, came to visit as did nurses from other floors who had cared for her in the past. Everyone was cheering her on, proud of her determination and impressed with her endurance; all except one doctor. This was a doctor we had not seen in the past, we barely saw during that admission and who we had very little conversation with because her demeanor had spoken volumes from the very beginning. She didn't seem the least bit interested in anything Brit or I had to say, though we found out later that apparently she was critiquing every word that came out of Britney's mouth. She had no use for any opinions from the many specialists, affiliated with her own hospital, or doctors who had treated Brit for the last nineteen years.

Because Britney's veins were so worn out her doctors, knowing that she was going to be taken into the OR for the abscess, kept requesting that a port be placed while she was already under sedation. Unfortunately, the doctor in charge of Brit's case happened to be nothing but a floor doctor with no history or familiarity with her case. Another thing that worked against us in this admission was that Britney's longtime cardiologist, one who had been affiliated with this hospital for over thirty years, recently had retired. Before his unplanned retirement, he had referred us to a cardiologist he trusted but who was affiliated with a different pediatric hospital. Unfortunately, he passed away soon after.

Because keeping Britney hydrated fell under cardiology, the floor doctor felt she needed a direct order from that specialist. Only, our new doctor couldn't dictate orders when she wasn't affiliated with the hospital we were admitted to. It didn't matter that Dr. Bryan, and several of Brit's other specialists, put in phone calls and emails; she was determined that Brit wasn't getting that port.

Still, the days dragged on, and it seemed like we were just there being monitored and receiving meds. Eventually, a bedside cardiac test was ordered and Brit had her IV fluids and pain meds discontinued to prepare for that test. She was miserable because her head, hurting from surgery, was almost unbearable as her heart rate fluctuated making it pound even worse. Without IV fluids, Brit's heart rate and blood pressure couldn't be regulated. It didn't matter that she already had a lot of fluids in her or that she was consuming large amounts orally; her body simply didn't absorb or retain fluids. It was a miserable two days but it was about to get worse.

The night before the test was to be administered, a new nurse came in to give Brit her nighttime meds. As she was reading them off, she listed one that caught both of our attention. It was a heart medication that Brit had taken if her heart rate was consistently above a certain number but it had never been given at this high of a dose. When Britney, with her famous "Well, actually", mentioned her heart rate wasn't where it needed to be to require the medication, the nurse listened. When I explained that the dose prescribed was also twice the strength she usually got, she paid attention. I also explained that, in order for the test to be accurate, that type of medication could not be given within twenty-four hours of the test. The nurse offered to hold the meds and ask her supervisor if it was okay to go ahead or hold them. The nurse in charge agreed that the medication should not be given and Britney took great delight in exercising her right to decline meds. That delight was short-lived because what we would face the next day, would not only pull our safety net out from under us, but it would leave Britney afraid of, and suspicious of, most doctors and medical facilities from that day forward.

The next morning, we found out that not only had the test been cancelled but, we were being discharged. We were excited to be able to go home and, after years of hospital life, we knew that since the orders had already been put in, we should be out of there before noon. Only we weren't.

The day dragged on and as the nurses would come in to check Brit, I noticed a change in the atmosphere. Our room had always been a room where the nurses would stay and visit, catch up on Brit's life and later play with Puppy. Suddenly, the nurse, as well as a tech, would come in and go out as quickly as possible and if they visited, it was vague and impersonal. Brit slept and I played on my phone trying to ignore the unease growing in the pit of my stomach. Soon the same caseworker who had handled Brit's discharges over many years came to our room. Only this time, she didn't give us papers to sign.

This time, she asked me to come with her. Brit immediately got a pensive look on her face but I assured her that it was likely a new policy because we were in the middle of the first round of COVID. I wasn't picking up on anything. This had been, from our point of view, one of our more anticlimactic admissions. We hadn't pushed for much and Brit's body hadn't thrown many surprises this time around. We had basically sat through ten mundane days getting the abscess cleaned out and waiting for the antibiotics to work and we were more than ready to get back to College Station. Maybe that's why, when the caseworker had me follow her down the hall and to another room, I didn't think much of it until we stopped in front of another patient room and she asked me to go in. When I stepped into that room, our medical life changed forever and we never let down our guard, or breathed easily, ever again.

I walked into a patient room that had been turned into a make-shift interrogation room. It was empty except for two chairs facing each other and a recording device. In one chair was a detective and the other chair was waiting for me.

The detective was kind, and I will always be thankful for that, but I didn't really care what was going on in this room. I was worried about Brit. I asked if I could send her a text telling her that I had a lot of paperwork to fill out and it may take a while and he allowed me to do that. Next, he asked me if I knew why I was there and, without even thinking, I voiced what had been one of my biggest fears since we had started this journey in healthcare. I said, "I can guess. I can guess because there isn't one of us that walks through these doors, on a regular basis, that isn't scared to death of this happening". He asked why I thought that and seemed genuinely curious. I never raised my voice, I never spoke condescendingly and I never disrespected him or the hospital but, I did tell the truth. "This hospital is known for what we are doing right now. I *do* realize it's necessary and I *do* realize that it does more good than harm. I *know* there are children that need to be protected, even from their own parents, and I wish I could help with all of them. Brit isn't one of them. You are welcomed to question her. She has Asperger's syndrome, and she won't lie, but you should be prepared for brutal truth. And, please don't think she's being rude. She just tells it like it is."

He never made me feel like a criminal, never made me feel intimidated and never was anything but pleasant and caring so, when he asked if he could see my phone, I handed it over. I told him he could look at everything. He read several weeks of texts between Brit and me and before long was chuckling and asking about her tortious, Puppy and Red. He asked about her days at college and we talked a little smack about where he had gone versus where Brit was attending. He asked about her medical history and I offered to sign anything he needed so that he could read her records. Looking back, I'm sure he could have accessed anything he needed to without my, or Brit's permission, but he said that wasn't necessary. He could see all he needed to see from our texts, and by questioning me, and what he saw was a girl who was going to college, living her dream, steadfast in her political views and loving her animals. That's all that was in Brit's texts to me. There was nothing about being sick, nothing about meds, nothing about pain. Just normal texts with the occasional "could you please help me" thrown in. He handed me his card, and said Adult Protection Services had been called but he would call and tell our caseworker that he saw no issues and wished us well.

When I got back to Britney's room, she informed me that a nice lady detective had questioned her but after three questions, which I have no doubt Brit answered very bluntly, they just played with Puppy and discussed guns. She wasn't bothered and I pretended I wasn't but on the inside, I was terrified. I knew everything could be proven with her records and I knew that, if I called Dr Bryan, he'd call her other doctors and have the issue settled but I was too scared to contact anyone. I had heard the stories from other parents and I knew what could happen. We sat there for several more hours before we were allowed to leave and through it all, I could barely breathe. I wouldn't leave her to go take Puppy to potty, I didn't take our bags to the car and I didn't call anyone or discuss anything with her because I was worried our room was bugged and if I moved wrong or said the wrong thing, they'd come in and take my daughter. I didn't do a thing but sit beside her and wait and that's pretty much what I did for the next few weeks.

I need to say that the nurses, our doctors and many others who had known us for years were all very supportive. I didn't tell any of them, except our closest medical family, but I didn't have to. Word got around and as it did, more and more people were furious and before long, the tides turned. I was the one trying to calm everyone down, the one not willing to pursue things to get us some justice and the one who ultimately took up for the doctor. Why I did that, I'll never know except I actually felt sorry for her. She was so haughty while being so incompetent and though she had worked for her degree, I imagined it took a lot on her part. I'm a doctor's daughter, and I was in my teens when my dad went to medical school, so I know the amount of work it takes and the stress it causes. I couldn't picture her with her smug face working her way through because she hadn't shown us anything for her to be smug about. I saw a young woman trying to work her way through school and most likely not having the confidence, or intelligence, to keep herself afloat with the normal amount of hard work. I could only picture her frustrated, exhausted and having to work even harder than most to make it through and then, when she held that diploma, forgetting all of that. Forgetting how hard it was and hinging her identity on that piece of paper and suddenly having a power that allowed her to hold her head up and wear that condescending aura with pride.

That wasn't the only reason I didn't go after her. My main reason, and most important one, was that Brit had a goal and that goal didn't involve questioning, depositions or days in court. That would have hindered her college career not to mention the amount of mental and emotional stress she would have endured. We did talk about it, and we both agreed, that we wouldn't waste our time on someone like her. We would stick to Brit's plan, stay focused on college and work to get her to the point where she could make her mark far better, and far bigger, than the one that doctor had left on us.

Still, Brit had lost her safety net. We couldn't go back to the place where she loved the nurses, the pre-op and post-op knew her every need, the cafeteria ladies knew her favorite cupcakes, the child life department knew her favorite interests and, most of all, where Brit's life had been saved a few years before. There was no rule saying we couldn't go back but we both knew we couldn't without fear or apprehension. We never stepped foot in those halls again but we did keep our trusted doctors. We continued to see Dr. Bryan and Brit did tele-visits with her other specialists. They knew what had happened, they knew how scared she was and they wanted so badly to make it right. Not just them. Her doctors all over the country, and locally, were furious but determined to do whatever they could to keep Brit going the best they could.

The problem of a hospital was exacerbated by COVID. Brit was an adult but had not been in an adult hospital and, at the time, if you had to go into an ER, you had to go alone. I had not had Brit declared officially disabled, because, in our eyes, she wasn't. The only way that I could accompany her into an ER was to legally have her declared disabled and I didn't feel that was fair to her. I knew she had a future and I knew that having her declared like that would follow her the rest of her life. For the type of degree she was getting, and the job that would follow, that could have hampered her. Had it been just a physical disability, that wouldn't have been as big of a setback but in order for me to get to accompany her, we would have had to list her as intellectually disabled and that could have caused issues down the road.

So, we were stuck if we needed a hospital. She couldn't go back to the one she had considered a home away from home but there was no way she could go into a strange, adult hospital alone. Thankfully, she had been into an adult surgery center close to home, many times, and knew the staff very well so, within a week of leaving the hospital, her cardiologist sent orders to a surgeon and Brit received her much-needed port. I was allowed in with her and it all went quickly and smoothly. By the next week, she was back in class. Even down at our apartment, I was constantly looking over my shoulder, constantly scared they would come take her and constantly trying to not let Brit know how shaken I was. That fear followed us to Cincinnati that summer where, once again, our fears were laid to rest.

Britney was taking summer classes and between tests, that the doctors were running, she didn't rest; she studied. She had been losing weight for a couple of months before we went to Cincinnati, and some of her doctors at home were worried that she had developed cancer. She was losing three to five pounds a week and no one could figure out why. The obvious suspicion was cancer but we were hoping for something much less serious. We were blessed to find out that she was cancer-free, but they couldn't explain the weight loss at the time. Later, after watching her labs change over the course of several weeks, they would find that her inability to absorb nutrients was the culprit. She was slowly starving. All of her tests were finally over and other than having to Botox her duodenum, to keep that section functioning as it should, there were no other invasive procedures. We were able to head back to Texas and we headed back with Brit knowing she had a safe place, even if it was a thousand miles away.

Not only had Brit been reassured, but her doctors there had taken the time to let me know that they fully supported us and were making sure that it was communicated to the appropriate people. Before we left Cincinnati, I received the final call from Adult Protection Services saying the case was closed. I still have a screen-shot of that text because I had asked her to send me a text confirming the case was closed after she called. I wanted proof to carry with me.

Summer classes were wrapped up and it was time to head back to College Station for the next semester. COVID-19 had colleges, along with the whole world, shut down and while this was a detriment to some, it worked in Britney's favor. Remote learning was something she had been forced to do for years so it didn't hinder her educationally or socially. It also allowed her to work around her many doctors' appointments and procedures.

Chapter 16

I know Dr. Q will do everything possible and she will bully everyone to get it done. Then if it doesn't go the way we want it to, she'll bully everyone to the end to make sure I am ok.
—Britney

Because the bulk of her doctors were affiliated with the hospital we no longer felt welcome in, most of Brit's appointments were done via tele-visit but she still saw Dr. Bryan. She also saw her doctors who were affiliated with other hospitals not only pediatric, but adult hospitals as well. I thought a doctor should lay eyes on her, examine her and record his or her professional evaluation into her chart. Being freshly accused of wrong-doing, I wanted professional documentation about her condition and what treatment she should be having. I would not make the mistake of being that trusting again and I would make sure that someone could not come along and accuse us of something like that ever again.

One of the first things I did was to get the CD with all of Brit's medical records from one hospital and then print out every user-name and password to every medical portal. I even printed out user-names and passwords to all of her lab portals. By doing this, I could hand it all over to a doctor both Brit and I trusted, knowing he could see it all. He wouldn't just be able to access all of her medical records, he'd be able to read any electronic communication between me and all medical staff. I had nothing to hide, Brit had nothing to hide and the only way for us to truly show that was to be completely open and transparent.

I took all of these records to Dr. T, a trusted doctor from her past. He was interested in reading all he could and becoming her primary doctor as she transitioned into adult care. We thought we had a while to prepare for this because Brit actually was showing a lot of progress. The abscesses were getting few and far between and her pain level had dropped so much that she had weaned off most of her medicines. Things were looking up and we were excited, but with COVID-19, came a new vaccine and being that Brit didn't have much of an immune system, we started researching it.

My gut said no but I left it up to Brit. She had many discussions with her doctors and I want to be clear that not one of them pushed it on her. While none of them felt that they could promise it could protect her, none of them felt it could harm her. She did her research and was on the fence about it but there were others who felt she and I were being stubborn by not getting the vaccine that they had gotten themselves. The vaccines were getting higher and higher in demand and it was getting closer to time for us to return to campus. Brit was worried we would get back to A&M, she'd get sick and it would ruin her whole semester. More than that, she was worried that with me being *older*, I would catch it even easier than she would. So, between being pressured to have the shot and worrying about what could happen, she decided to get the first round of the vaccine and she asked me to get it too.

Within the first few hours, we both had sore arms but other than that, I had no side effects. Brit, on the other hand, spiked a fever and we couldn't get it down. Then her joints started swelling, she got a streaky rash and her eyes became horribly bloodshot. Within twelve hours of that shot, she had gone from being almost a *'typical'* college student with a bright future, to right back where she had been when we started this journey nineteen years before. Only this time, she wouldn't respond to any of the treatments we had given her years before. At this point, Brit had entered into a decline that she would never pull out of, leaving me with the biggest "What if?" of my life.

Because Dr. Bryan was a pediatrician, and switching to adult care was being forced on to us as Brit was in a health decline, we had to decide which adult doctor we could trust. It was with Dr. Bryan's blessing, and without a doubt or any hesitation, that we had handed all of these records over to Dr. T. We didn't know that we would be needing his knowledge so quickly but I am so thankful we had already put our trust in him as Brit's primary physician. He had been Brit's immunologist over the years but, because she'd had some better years, she hadn't seen him as a patient in some time. She had kept up communication with him because he was now her fellow Aggie, not just her doctor.

Dr. T was thrilled to have Brit back but not thrilled that she was in such a decline. He went through all her records, ordered his own tests, saw her many times in his office and did the very best he could for her. More importantly, he continued to build a friendship and develop a trust with Britney and before long, she did her tele-visits with him on her own. He encouraged her to keep on with her college work and celebrated each accomplishment with her, and there were many. Brit only had tele-visits with him when we were in College Station and she would show him all of her Aggie memorabilia and share whatever assignment she was working on. It was only fitting that after she was gone, I gifted him a large collection of her meticulous notes. I knew that she would trust that only he would be able to comprehend and appreciate those notes. Her notes and some of that cherished memorabilia are now displayed in his office.

Dr. T was a huge asset in so many ways, one being that he treated both pediatric and adult cases. More importantly, he is brilliant and highly respected throughout the medical community. His knowledge and experience are counterbalanced by his humbleness and quiet demeanor. His cowboy boots and casual attire were comfort to Britney over the typical sterile scrubs. He was a familiar, trusted figure in Brit's healthcare but he also became her bridge into the adult realm of medical care. Between Dr. T and Dr. Marc, Brit was well taken care of and always in the background, was Dr. Bryan watching over it all and guiding everyone along. Switching to adult care wasn't our only change in the medical world. Jan had retired and, though we were sad to see her leave the office, she had more free time to just be a friend. That became invaluable as Brit started slipping into an even more steady decline.

By now Brit was doing all of her classes online, as were the rest of her peers, and she and I spent our time at our apartment in College Station or living in my parents' guesthouse. I went to work and Brit did her classes on her own but with someone always close by and readily available if she needed anything. I was working for Dr. Q, a close friend, my doctor of twenty-five years and Brit's doctor for the last six years. Dr. Q had delivered Brit twenty years earlier and for the last ten years had become like an aunt to both of my children.

There were days that Brit was struggling too much to be left by herself so she would accompany me to work and rest in the break room. I was so busy trying to keep our lives together that I didn't see what was happening right in front of my face. I did notice that Brit was rapidly losing weight once again, but she had a good appetite so I didn't really worry about it. She was happy and more outgoing than she had been in years so when people were around her, that was what they noticed. We all did. We all noticed that for the first time ever, she enjoyed socializing and would visit without being prompted to.

It was Dr. Q who first brought the massive weight loss to my attention. I countered her with the fact that Brit seemed to have more life in her than she ever had. That was when she said, "Y'all are always so hopeful, and I think that is great, but hope can become a detriment when it clouds your judgment". She went on to say that she felt, that even though Brit was eating large amounts of calories, she was not absorbing any of it so her body was starting to eat itself. When the body does this, the muscles are the first to go and our hearts are a muscle so now, her heart was being affected more directly than ever.

Over the next few weeks, we watched her labs and then made the decision to try TPN (total parenteral nutrition) once again. This meant bi-weekly bloodwork, appointments with several different specialists, long phone calls with the pharmacy formulating her TPN and weekly visits with Dr. Q. Sometimes these visits were in her office and sometimes she had to come to the parking lot to assess Britney in the car because she was too weak to go in. Brit was being monitored by home health but, because we had lived this life for so long, the bulk of the care was on our shoulders. We had our routine and routines were how Britney functioned best. We started each morning by stepping on the scales then dipping her urine to check to see how her kidneys were functioning.

Even if we hadn't had the lab reports from her bloodwork and the urine samples we took in, to be sent off with her blood, it was apparent that her body was shutting down and we both knew it. We didn't discuss it. We just kept going and kept thinking that she would turn around as she had so many times before. Then one day her lab results came back and we couldn't deny what was happening any longer. Getting nutrition from TPN is a last resort. Most times, TPN is a lifesaver, as it had been for her in the past, but this time, not even that worked. Britney's body was shutting down, her organs were failing and there was nothing any of us could do.

We still had hope and no matter how many lab results I saw, how many doctors told me how bad things were or how many friends tried to reach out, I couldn't wrap my mind around it. I got the call about the latest lab results with Dr. Q saying, "There will be no more tests and no more TPN ordered", not because we didn't want to keep trying but because we weren't helping. We also knew that to continue to pump her full of TPN and fluids could only make things worse, though it didn't seem things could get any worse.

I didn't tell Brit. I made her dinner, helped her get settled with her iPad and said I had to run to the store. Only I didn't. I did something I was just beginning to learn to do. I made a phone call and ran to the person who would be right beside me from that day on and, right beside Brit until she drew her last breath. I had never run to anyone when things were tough. We had been blessed with several people we were very close to, and they were more than willing to support, but I had been the type to shoulder whatever needed to be shouldered on my own. I was there to support Brit and my needs were of no concern to me and frankly, it was easier to ignore my emotions or feelings. If we were up against a lot of odds, there were a handful I might call and vent to, and of course I always let Ms. C and Mrs. Brady know, but there had been very few times I had let my guard down and leaned on anyone. But then again, I hadn't been at this point before and, there are some people who come into your life, decide what their place is and, no matter how stubborn you've always been, you don't argue.

Brit and I had met Carla four months before when the kids and I were staying at my parents during Brit's dad's bout with COVID. Brit wasn't the type to quit what she was doing and seek out conversation with very many people. She was mannerly and would acknowledge anyone who spoke to her, and she would even offer the first hello at times, but she didn't go out of her way to initiate a conversation. We were sitting in my parents' living room one evening when Carla came by to drop something off. We had heard about her for years, because my parents were friends with her and her husband, but the person we'd heard about did not, in anyway, match the stories we'd heard.

We'd heard funny stories, from my mom, about traveling out of the country with Carla and even more stories about the things she said over dinner or while playing Rummikub. It was from these stories that I had formed an image of a larger than life woman with a domineering presence, likely tall and not mousy. So, when this short little spitfire walked into my parents' house, she wasn't at all like I thought she'd be though, later I learned, stature has no bearing on whether you have a domineering presence or are larger than life. She was both, but all wrapped up in a very small package with eyes that twinkled when happy, and spat fire when not, and the best laugh you've ever heard. Not only did her appearance not fit the stories we'd heard, neither did her transportation. She rode up on a bicycle and was unstrapping her bright orange helmet as she rang the doorbell. With the other hand, she was holding a Yeti cup that was keeping the martini, she'd made me, nice and cold.

This entire first impression was made in a matter of seconds but that's all the time she needed and what happened next left us all talking later. Brit was sitting on the couch hooked up to her IV fluids and reading on her iPad but after Carla started talking, she put her iPad down and started paying attention. Then, Carla said something about Mars and Brit got up, carried her bag of fluids along with the pump, walked over to where we were standing in the entryway and started talking. She talked and talked then, talked some more. She gave us all a textbook's worth of information about Mars and before long, I was trying to get Brit's attention to give her the signal that we were beating a subject to death. A dissertation that had started with a quick glance at me and her famous "Well, actually".

Only, Brit wasn't looking at me for her cues like she usually did. She wasn't looking at the floor or off in the distance; she was looking right at Carla and she was smiling as she talked. After a while, I started trying to figure out how to discreetly get Brit's attention, only I didn't really have to worry because soon Carla's eyes were glazing over and at the first chance she got she said, "Well, you sure know a lot about Mars and I think it's interesting but, after all of that, I need a drink!". And somehow, standing in that entryway, during a dissertation about Mars, a bond was formed and it was a bond that somehow gave Brit the comfort she needed when she made some tough decisions that August and then later, when she had to let go.

Chapter 17

I don't want any crying and no hanging over me looking like everything is terrible. I want to only have the people here that I want here and no other visitors. I want to lay up here and read by myself. When I know I'm about to lose consciousness, I'll tell you and then you can come up here and stay. I know I'll be unaware to a degree but please don't forget I'm still on the autism spectrum and no matter how out of it I am, I WILL know if there are other people here or ya'll are trying to touch me.

I want to talk to a minister and I need a lawyer so I can leave instructions. I'm not scared but that doesn't mean I like it and I still don't understand why God put this brain in this body. I will be asking about that.

Will you be ok? If you want me to keep trying I will but it will be useless and I'll just have to go through more tubes and tests. If it would help, I would try but I'd rather be honest and do this the way I want to.

—Britney

While I was working, Steph stayed with Brit when she could and on the other days, my parents or Carla were always available. Before long, I'd get a text saying that Carla was picking Brit up or they were going to get a snow cone, work on a puzzle or any other thing they came up with. Then, when Brit started getting sicker and I quit work to stay home with her, at some point every day, there would be a knock at the door. That visit usually came with a stuffed animal for Brit and some kind of food for me and that continued through a bout of pneumonia for me and starting TPN for Brit.

One day, when she knocked on the door, I was ready for her. Brit was upstairs and couldn't hear us and I started in on the spiel that I had laid out for many others. "You may not want to get too close. She's sicker than she's ever been and I worry that, if you get too close, you will end up hurting if she doesn't pull through. What about your family and your husband? Don't they need you? What about your friends and the ladies you play games with? You can't be taking up all of your time with us."

My spiel was pointless. I was met with a nonchalant, "Well aren't I lucky to have you here to make decisions for me. You aren't going to do this alone so hush up. Now that settles that." And, it did. Oh, I pushed back. I found every reason that I didn't need help. We were a burden, we were too much and the list goes on. I even played the snarky card, the one where I get all cool and aloof and not very easy to be around but, the harder I pushed, the less ground I covered. Sometimes I was beyond grateful but most of the time I was scared and worried that Carla would end up hurt so I'd start pushing back again. Steph had a front-row seat and found it highly entertaining that I had finally met my match with someone could so effortlessly put me in my place. She'd laugh and laugh at our battle of the wills and then talk sense into me later. Regardless of how scared I was, I wouldn't have taken the comfort of Carla's presence away from Britney no matter what kind of price any of us might have to pay if we truly couldn't turn this downhill slide around.

I'll never know, or even begin to guess, what drew Britney to Carla. They were about as opposite as you can get and Brit, having very little patience for anyone not on her same level, had never shown this kind of attachment to anyone. Before long, she asked if she could text Carla if she needed anything while I wasn't home and then, she asked to go stay with her one day. Brit's idea of a perfect friendship had always been someone who didn't like to talk but if they had to, she liked them to stick to the facts and know their business on a level far above one that any of us would care about. Carla could list her facts but her accuracy wasn't quite on a level that Brit would have approved of. Still, she somehow became Britney's favorite person and one day I couldn't help myself. I had to ask what it was about her that made Brit love her so much. Brit answered, "Well, I don't know. Most people like her drive me insane. When you try to talk to her about something, it's like being on a carousel and riding a roller coaster at the same time but, I just like her."

One evening, Brit and I were alone. I had just switched out her bags of TPN and hung a new bag of IV fluids when she said, "Are you okay with me going on hospice?" She said it like she was asking if I wanted pizza for dinner and I was thankful I was putting clean sheets on my bed so I could turn my back to her. Every part of me was screaming, "No, I am *not* okay with you going on hospice and why can't I crawl in bed with you for a little while and watch a movie? Can't we pretend this isn't happening?" But then I remembered that Brit's mind didn't work like mine. She didn't operate on emotions; she operated on facts. That doesn't mean that she didn't have emotions or that she was a robot. Brit had empathy and compassion far beyond what most of us experience but these decisions didn't involve a lot of feelings for her because, when it was all said and done, there really wasn't room for feelings. She had her facts and the science behind them and if she was going to have to face what all of the facts were showing her, she wanted to do it on her terms. So, I calmly said, "If that's what you think we need to do, that's what we will do" with pretty much the same tone I'd have used had I said that pizza was the perfect choice for dinner.

Then, I stumbled down the stairs and called Dr. Q, who said she'd be over the next evening to talk with her. At that time, I still expected one of Brit's famous turn-arounds and I really hoped that, after talking with Dr. Q, Brit would decide to try something else but, once again, Brit was ahead of me. She had accepted the facts, she knew what was coming and she told Dr. Q what she knew needed to happen. Dr. Q told her to think about it over the weekend and be in her office at nine o'clock Monday morning.

As requested, Britney spent time upstairs with some close family friends that Saturday, a minister and his wife. I don't know what all was said, because I let her have her privacy with them, but I do know that Brit was sure of where she was going and was confident in being reunited with us one day. She had questions about the in between, the time that her heart stopped and she actually stepped through heaven's gates. She was scared, and it still breaks my heart to know that she bore that fear and faced it head-on, not wanting to lay any of it on us, though we'd have gladly helped her carry it.

Sunday came and I was dreading Monday. Carla had been going to all of Brit's appointments with us but that evening, Brit asked me to ask her not to go the next morning. She was worried that it would hurt her to witness Brit making her decision and she didn't want to lay that on her. So, I asked her not to go but to meet us back at the house when we got home.

I'll never forget that day, the drive, the appointment, the drive back home and the desperation I felt but couldn't show. I wanted Brit to not just know, but to feel, fully supported in her decision. I wanted her not to worry about the pain or sadness I might feel and to not worry about anyone else, just her.

We got to the doctor's office and shuffled inside. Brit was in her wheelchair, Puppy on her lap and her TPN, along with a pump, was in a backpack hanging from the back of her chair. I had a purse slung across me, a folder of Brit's papers and a bag of IV fluids that I was holding between my teeth as I navigated Brit's chair into the office.

I had just finished working a couple of months in this office and many of those days, Britney was with me. They all knew her and they all knew me. They also knew why we were there and I wish I hadn't put that on them. More importantly, I wish I hadn't let Dr. Q take the role that she took. No matter how many years she'd been a doctor, Brit was her mini me, her friend and her family. She'd brought her into this world and was the first to catch her and listen to her lungs, and now… she was sitting quietly in a room with Brit and me, trying to calmly explain what hospice meant and listening to her heart and lungs for the last time.

As much as I hated for Dr. Q to do this, I knew that Britney needed her to be the one to do it. Brit trusted Dr. Q on a level that she didn't trust any of her other doctors possibly, because she was part of our family and spent countless hours in our home closely involved in my children's lives. Knowing Brit, I think the real reason was that she thought Dr. Q was one of the smartest women she'd ever known. She often remarked, "It's nice to have someone intelligent to talk to", when I would tell her Dr. Q was coming over to visit. They were a lot alike in their thoughts and opinions and Britney was right in feeling that Dr. Q was on the same level that she was when it came to intelligence. Britney was truly more like Dr. Q than she was like me and they shared a deep connection. I've always jokingly said that it must have come from my prenatal care but the truth is, I'm proud that my daughter was so much like her.

Brit knew what hospice meant and knew that it didn't always mean imminent death but meant no more treatment, just comfort care. Dr. Q went over all of this along with the fact that there would be no more blood tests, tubes or intervention and, when this batch of TPN ran out, there would be no more delivered. She asked Brit if she understood and that's when Britney finally spoke and asked, "How long?" to which she responded that she imagined it would be one to maybe three weeks. That's when Brit's resolve broke and she cried. It was gut-wrenching but for the first time, and after I asked permission, she let me hug her to comfort her. I remember not knowing what to say. I hadn't thought to this point, hadn't come up with any wise words or rehearsed how I would act so, I just said what I always said, "We will get through this". "We will. We will do it the way you want it done and we will do it so well that others, coming behind us, will want to know how we did it so they can do it just as well. I hate it, I hate it for you, but we will do it and we will do it better than it's ever been done," and right then and there, that became my plan. Had I known then, what I would know a few weeks later, that still would have been my plan but I would have been much more prepared for the reality that hit us.

That's not true. Nothing can prepare you to watch your child die but you can read all the pamphlets hospice gives you and try to prepare yourself. Brit didn't follow any of the patterns that I read about. The patterns that I read about were peaceful and somewhat predictable. Nothing about Britney's transition into eternity was peaceful or predictable. She had to suffer and fight to live her life and, she would have to suffer and fight to pass from it.

We left Dr. Q's office and Brit wanted to stop by Chick-fil-A to get her favorite biscuits. We did, and we ordered ten. Neither of us could eat and when I looked in the rearview mirror, she had fallen asleep with a tear falling down one cheek and the other lying on one of Carla's shirts that had been left in our car. When we pulled into the driveway at home, Carla pulled in behind us and she visited with Brit while I made two of the hardest phone calls I've ever made. First, I met my dad on their back porch to deliver the news and ask which hospice company he recommended. Then he got hold of the company for me while I called Brit's father and then, Zach. Calling them wasn't hard just because of the nature of the call; it was hard because it felt like failure. It felt like we had lost a battle and, though we hadn't given up, we were being forced to give in. Next, I called the same person I had called through every stressful situation involving Brit, Jan. I called her and she said she'd be over and would stay while hospice came to do their evaluation and she did.

When the hospice nurse came, she didn't realize she'd be admitting such a young patient and she certainly didn't realize she'd be evaluating one who was so wise. It was surreal to sit beside my twenty-year-old daughter while she laid out her plans and ultimately educated that young nurse. Carla and Jan were standing across the room and had they not been there, I'm sure it would have been even more unbelievable. Brit was very specific with the nurse and even paused now and then to make sure the nurse was writing everything down. I don't remember much of what Brit told her but I do remember her requesting a DNR and then telling us all that she had her other DNR in her medical folder downstairs.

I also remember Brit specifically asking her to write down that she wanted to be cremated and she was worried that, after she was gone, we may try to change her plans. She told the nurse that she didn't want to be put under the dirt, that she had never liked being that close to people and that, frankly, she felt our cemeteries were getting overcrowded. She sat there and said it in her matter-of-fact way and when the nurse asked her did she realize that there would be no more treatment, Britney replied, "Well, duh, I'm on hospice. I wouldn't expect treatment when I'm dying."

I can tell you what sheets were on her bed, what clothes we all had on and the color of the nurses scrub's but I can't tell you how it felt. There are no words to explain it. It's hard on all of us moms when our children, no matter how grown they are, make a big decision. Those decisions come in many forms; moving out, changing jobs, deciding on a college far from home, joining the military or a host of many other things that we have to let them do on their own. Sitting with your twenty-year-old daughter as she goes over the plans for the final days of her life, is a whole different scenario. Those other decisions follow the natural order but nothing about losing a child, no matter how old they are, is natural in any way, shape or form.

At this point, Britney was still on TPN even though we knew it wasn't working. She was also on the highest volume of IV fluids that could be given but she was still dehydrated because she wasn't absorbing anything at all. She knew that nothing was working but she didn't want to just suddenly stop everything. She wanted to finish off this shipment of TPN and then bring her fluids down slowly in hopes that she would just fall asleep. Even though she had made her decision and knew that there wasn't anything we could possibly do, she was still a little scared and a little hesitant to hurry into the unknown.

So, we did it her way and she bravely led us through it step by step until she lost consciousness. The night that we finished that last bag of TPN, and I turned off that pump for the last time, I truly thought I was going to lose my mind. Not Brit. She had me unhook her fluids and took what would be her very last shower. I remember carrying her up the stairs and trying to concentrate on the smell of her hair instead of the fact that she would never go down the stairs again. I wanted to remember how she smelled because I was scared I would forget.

I knew that we needed to start turning the IV fluids down or we were going to run out and to stop them suddenly would have caused a lot of extra stress on her body. I didn't want to remind her and I knew if I did it without telling her, she would notice. I didn't have to do either one, because when Britney climbed back into that bed she said, "Momma, you need to turn those fluids down". Every day after that, she would quietly remind me again that it was time to turn them down even more. Then, before I knew it, it was time to pull that needle out of her chest for the last time. There were no more fluids and she would never need her port again.

Chapter 18

Love you too!

—*Britney*

Through all of this, Brit still wanted to be left to herself to read or watch stuff on her iPad. Honoring her wishes was one of the hardest things I did and to this day, the thought of her lying up there by herself torments me. I understood why she wanted to be alone, why she didn't want visitors and why she needed time to herself. We had lived with autism all of her life but she had overcome so much of it, that I often forgot that she still very much had those tendencies. Brit didn't forget, and she was very clear on not wanting visitors, not wanting any sadness or crying around her and exactly who she wanted to be with us during this time. When I would go upstairs to check on her, I'd always ask if she was ready for me to sit with her and she always let me know that when she was, she would tell me. I wanted so badly to be up there with her but I also knew that this was the last thing I could do for her and I was going to do it exactly how she wanted me to.

Brit asked that only Steph, Carla, Dr. Q and I stay close. I know that all three of them brought her comfort but I don't think that's why she chose them. I think that, as much as I wanted to help Britney get through this, she was focused on helping me get through it and she chose the perfect ones to help me through. Somehow, without even realizing it, we fell into a routine of Steph keeping us well fed, helping me with Brit as needed and taking care of any need we had. We had set up a monitor so we could watch Brit when we weren't upstairs and if Steph wasn't busy, she was watching that monitor so I could get a few minutes of sleep here and there. She talked sense into me when I was irrational and showed up with my favorite treats to try to coax me to eat. Steph had been a comfort to Brit for many years and if I couldn't be by her bed, Steph was. We had worked side by side for so long that I didn't have to ask; she just knew. I know Brit was more comfortable with her there and I know I couldn't have focused on Brit like I did if she hadn't been there to take care of all of the mundane.

Dr. Q played two roles, the first being our close friend and comforter but also the second, her role as a doctor. I don't think I gave one dose of medicine without asking her even though I knew exactly how to do it. We were in new territory and somehow I questioned every step I took. I only knew how to fight to keep Britney alive so with every new symptom, my default was to fix it and find an answer. Dr. Q had to continually remind me that we weren't there to fix, but to comfort. Being that she isn't only my friend, but my doctor of twenty-five years, she not only watched out for Brit, she watched out for me too. Dr. Q was who I looked to when I needed the hard things said out loud so that I could try to comprehend them. She was the one I needed to remind me that we had truly done all we could do and no amount of pushing on my part could change that. I couldn't have found the small amount of peace I had, about Brit's decision, if it hadn't been for her. I fully trusted her, and still do, and I knew she was on top of everything medical. I also knew, that no matter how much I may have argued, she was taking care of me and I couldn't have made it through with the small shred of sanity that I still had, had it not been for her.

Carla's role was pretty much a constant change of hats. She was a source of comfort to both Brit and me but also entertainment for Brit when she was awake and aware. She took on the role of a coordinator when it came to any visitors, my sleeping and eating, making sure we didn't have to deal with the world outside our walls and over all doing what the rest of us didn't have the guts to. When I would waver on some of Brit's instructions, because I was overly conscious of others, she held fast reminding me that nothing, besides doing our best for Brit, mattered. When she wasn't leaning over Brit's bed, she was leaning over me, sometimes holding my water to my mouth or pinching off bites of food and putting them in my mouth. She was a force to be reckoned with that was only surpassed by the care and love she showed. I know that Brit would have fought to hang on had she not known Carla was there to take care of me.

That was the four of us. Just us, and Brit, along with the very few she wanted to see. My dad was fighting his second round of COVID, and I know it was hard for my parents to be right across the backyard but not be able to visit. At the same time, I'm so thankful they didn't have to watch her walk through the last leg of her journey or watch me go through it. I know it was hard on so many to not be there in person to offer support, but that's not what Brit wanted and I think she knew that it was not what I needed.

There were some who Brit let come visit out of consideration for them. She was at her most vulnerable and only wanted those who had been right beside her through every obstacle she had had to face. I was proud of her for being considerate and I knew she did this out of her love for those she let visit. We kept those visits short because Britney knew she was running out of energy and there were a few she wanted to save her strength for.

Cindy Tilton - not Ms. Cindy and not Mrs. Tilton, only the name Cindy Tilton would do in Brit's world. Cindy Tilton came regularly and Brit enjoyed those visits with her as much as she had enjoyed her company at FFA functions and at the new church we were attending. Cindy Tilton's boys were a part of FFA, through Britney's high school years, and Tanner was really special to her.

Mrs. Cindy Tilton was one of the very few that Britney allowed to hug and kiss on her and she continued to come and shower Brit with that affection long after our girl was aware of anyone's presence. It was after one of those visits that Cindy and I sat and went over the plans Brit had written for her funeral. The last and final plans. The ones that didn't differ a whole lot from the previous plans except there would be no blue casket or hay bales. These plans were much more centered around the message she wanted portrayed, the music she had picked, those she wanted to speak and still, for momma to sit by Ms. C. She wanted Tanner to say a prayer, she wanted the Aggie War Hymn for a recessional, no flowers and something simple at the Baptist Church she now called home.

She wanted to see Jan, and Jan came, with the same calming reassurance she had brought us for the last twenty years. She not only brought comfort to Britney, but her soft voice and her famous hugs brought the same comfort to me that they had for many years. When Jan was there, I could breathe. Not only did she bring emotional support, but being a nurse, I could run my never-ending list of questions by her. She had known Brit longer than anyone else in that guest house and she knew more about Britney's medical history than I could recall with my sleep- deprived mind. I was still questioning myself and still trying to be sure that we had tried everything we possibly could so her quiet reassurance did more for me than I can put into words.

Of course Britney wanted to see Zachary and their dad, and they came, but she was starting to slip away and she knew it. She would rouse for them but it took a lot out of her to interact. When Jan and Cindy came, she didn't always rouse, so their visits weren't taxing to her. They had already said what they wanted to say and she knew she could lie there and sleep while Cindy Tilton and Jan were content just to sit by her and look at her beautiful face.

She wanted to rouse and visit with her brother and dad but she was very concerned that she save her energy for one last visit with two very important people. She did get in a good visit with one other very special person, and that was an evening that she rallied, but soon after, she started fading so I made the call that I had been dreading. I called Ms. C and Mrs. Brady and told them it was time to get in one last visit, while she was still a little aware, and they made plans to come that evening.

That morning, Brit said she'd like for me to come up there and stay. When I got up there, she let me crawl in bed with her and asked if Carla would come up too. After reassuring her that I would wake her up when her visitors came, Britney laid her head on my chest and went to sleep. She was in and out of consciousness all day and when she would rouse, she would remind me to make sure that she stayed awake to see Ms. C. and Mrs Brady. I'm thankful to say that I got to lie there with her for two whole days. I took a break during that much-needed visit but resumed my spot as soon as they left. I stayed there until her autism reared its ugly head, in the middle of the night, and she sent me, along with the bed rail, right across the floor. Brit had been right; even being barely conscious, her senses were still hyper vigilant and she still didn't want to be touched.

Over the years, we had been through many of these visits with Ms. C and Mrs. Brady. Many times with these visits we thought it may be the last but this time, we knew it would be and there was no avoiding it. We all put our brave faces on and skirted around reality as I took them upstairs to see Brit. I woke her up and she smiled when she saw them. She had asked me to keep her awake so I had to coax her every now and then. She didn't open her eyes much, but she did talk some, and it was during a conversation with Mrs. Brady that I saw Brit shed the only tear she let slip during her final days. She said, "I'm not going to get my Aggie ring" and a single tear rolled down her cheek.

For fifteen years, these two ladies had showered all the love and affection that Britney would allow on her. They had cheered her on through the good and bad, advocated for her, met her every need and during it all, spoiled her as only they could. Now they were here for the awful and they were doing it the best way they possibly could have. They were holding back their tears, telling her about things they knew would interest her and getting a faint grin out of her now and then, all the while watching for that next breath. I know that Britney knew that they were hurting, and I know she wanted to give something back, something special that they could hold onto.

As they said their goodbyes, they both leaned down to hug and kiss her and tell her they loved her. We all tried to laugh and say things about it being the first time she wasn't trying to avoid the affection but the gravity of it all was weighing us down and, for a minute, we all just stood there quietly and watched her rest. She seemed to have slipped back into sleep but just as they got to her door, she said, "I love you too". I have no doubt that Brit had been wanting to say that for years and now she had given those words to them as a gift. It was her way of showing a little of the love they had poured into her.

After they left, Steph made her pallet on the couch downstairs while Carla and I made our way upstairs to what had become our new normal. Our normal night was Carla asleep in my twin bed, about four feet from

Brit, with me sitting beside Brit's bed sometimes dozing but most of the time not. Sometimes I lay on the floor beside Brit and sometimes I slept in that twin bed with Carla. We were all going through the motions, living from minute to minute, waiting, watching and trying to make it through.

Nights were extra long because from about midnight to five in the morning, Brit would get restless and oftentimes combative. Everything in me wanted to crawl in that bed and just hold her and there were a few stretches where I was able to but, for the most part, any touching or talking sent her into a confused, combative state and that just added to her suffering. During the day, she would sleep peacefully for the most part but only with a loud fan and a sound machine going. Any stimulation, even whispering with the nurse, sent her over the edge. If she got to this point, she'd come up off the bed and try to walk only to collapse onto the floor.

By now, she had lost her sight and she was so thin that I could scoop up all five foot seven inches of her and lay her back in bed like an infant. The days dragged into weeks and each day, we met new obstacles that I won't go into because I still want to preserve Brit's dignity. No medicines helped, though we continued to give them as scheduled. She couldn't absorb nutrients or fluids and she wasn't absorbing the liquid meds we were putting under her tongue or in her cheeks. Brit's brilliant brain would not shut down, though her body and her mind had. She would beg for water, but when we gave it, she couldn't swallow. She would whimper and say, "Momma, I think I'm sick again" but wouldn't understand anything I tried to tell her or be soothed by my touch.

This is how we lived for days on end. We would all get up and stumble to the coffee pot in shifts so that Brit wasn't left alone. During the week, Steph went on grocery runs, cooked food, did laundry and anything else she could to help. Between five and seven, Carla took my phone, Steph took her post with Brit and I was urged to try to sleep or at least lie down. Most evenings, Dr. Q would come after work often with dinner in hand. Carla would go home for maybe an hour to shower only to come right back to take up her spot again. Often, she, Dr. Q and Steph would play Rummikub or Phase10 while I sat with Brit or tried to catch a nap. Sometimes I'd sit down there with them, answering texts and calls and watching the monitor so, if Brit came up out of the bed, I could try to get up the stairs and catch her before she fell.

For the most part, evenings were calm. Though we kept as much white noise going as we could, Brit somehow knew when the garage door would go up and Carla would leave to go home to shower and see Bill for a short time. Britney generally would spend the hour that Carla was gone restless and agitated. There were times I'd have to lie on her to keep her from trying to come out of that bed. As soon as Carla got back, she would calm down and rest. These were the times Brit slept most soundly so if we got a chance, we four would have dinner together, try to visit and even attempt to find some humor. Sometimes, if we could manage a laugh, it would send us almost into hysterics and this was dangerous ground. Laughter is an emotion and oftentimes our laughter would result in uncontrolled tears on my part. The pressure of each long day was getting to all of us and it was starting to show.

Chapter 19

Thank you Mommy!

—Britney

Every day seemed to fly by as we were dragging through it. Every day, she suffered more and I remember during one of the times I was able to lie in her bed and hold her, I begged God to take her. To take her home and free her from the suffering. This was the part we hadn't bargained for. We had nothing to compare to, being that we hadn't been around anyone as they were dying. We both thought it would be peaceful, that we would all be sitting with her and soothing her as she passed. It wasn't that way at all.

It was around this time that I started to worry about Puppy. While he had been her greatest source of comfort over the last three years, she had also been his. He was still doing his job comforting and loving on his girl only his girl, as he had known her, was no longer there. When Britney was aware, she would reach out and pet him but when she got combative, she didn't know who he was and I could see that this was causing him a great deal of stress. When it became apparent that Brit was most likely not going to have control over her mind or emotions any longer, I knew it was time to let him retire and rest. All of us cried a little as Steph loaded him in her car and took him to some close friends he knew well and who would love on him until I came to him a week later.

Brit had to struggle to live and the ugly truth is, she had to struggle to die. I don't know that I will ever be able to reconcile that in my mind or heart. There was no gathering around her and softly telling her all the things we wanted to say. We couldn't even talk or she got agitated, even if we talked among ourselves.

When her dad and brother came, we had to sit in silence and when Dr. Q was there, I'd have to text Brit's vitals to her even though she was standing three feet away from me.

Soon, I lost track of time, days and weeks. The only difference between the weekends and the weekdays was that Friday night and Saturday night, Dr. Q was on the air mattress downstairs with Steph and then, as things progressed, upstairs with us. We fell into a routine, a survival mode and, we got through. What we went through, and the parts of us that left with Britney, will forever tie us four together almost like I can imagine soldiers feel after returning from battle. We were in a battle. It wasn't a battle fought with an urge to win; we weren't going to win, and we knew it. It was a battle to keep things as calm and comforting as we possibly could, and to do whatever it took, to help our girl transition into heaven as peacefully as possible.

Just as she had in living her life Brit, in her final days, did nothing by the book. She literally didn't do one thing in order or in the manner that hospice had told us to watch for. She would go from her coloring being nonexistent and breathing so shallow that we had to feel her chest for movement, to this rosy-cheeked, pink-lipped angel that couldn't possibly be sick. She hadn't spoken in days when all of the sudden, she pointed to the corner of the room and said she could see Red's herd and she wanted to go see him.

Thinking surely this must be it, I started telling her it was okay to go to him and she could ride all she wanted to. She said she had his bridle and she was going, only she didn't. She talked for a bit and was as clear as she had been weeks before. She told me that she was sorry and, when I managed to swallow the lump in my throat, I told her there was nothing on earth she should be sorry for. I told her how proud her dad and I were of her, how much Zach loved her and what a good sister she had been. How proud her doctors were of her and how proud everyone who knew her was. I told her how she had touched so many and that she was leaving a mark on this world that most people would never achieve and when I was done, she said, "I really thought we would beat this", and I told her we had. I told her that she had beat it by doing everything on her terms, by not letting it define her and living above any limitation life had tried to throw at her.

Then she went quiet and just lay there. After a bit, Carla asked her if she saw angels and she said yes and tried to describe them and again, I thought, *This must be it* and *I should call her dad and Zach.* But then, Carla asked her what she was going to do when she was an angel. That was when she got that little smirk she was so famous for and said, "Watch over my momma when you are driving," and then … I was hopeful enough to think maybe this was all a mistake. Maybe she was going to turn around after all. Only that night, and from then on, there were no restless nights, just deep sleep and no noise except a struggle to breathe every now and then. Even then, her breathing never became what we were warned to watch for and because of this, we all breathed a little easier and I started hoping that maybe she was going to prove us all wrong. Maybe we should keep that lease going at our apartment in College Station. Maybe I should contact her adviser and let her know that I'd get a note from her doctors explaining that she needed to sit out this semester but she would be back for the spring term. Brit's body was confirming exactly what we knew and discounting every hope I had, but still…

Dr. Q came over the evening before she left to visit her out- of-state grandkids and we all truly believed Brit would still be here when she got back. The next day, I even dared to raise the shades and turn one of the loud fans off and then was so impressed when Brit didn't get overstimulated. Zachary left for a leadership conference with his church group but took his truck in case he needed to return. We had a quiet day and quiet night that I should have slept through but didn't because I just wanted to look at her. To watch her sleep. To soak her in. I wanted to lean down and smell how she still smelled like she did when she was a baby, to try to get some of the tangles out of that thick, curly hair and make sure the heating pad stayed on her feet that I couldn't get warm.

The next day was calm and peaceful. When I went to lift Brit back up onto her pillows, she quietly said, "Thank you, Mommy". She had never called me mommy, not even as a child, but she did that day and those were the last words she ever spoke. The day went on and there was no change. The weekend nurse came and Brit's vitals weren't showing much change from the days before and she said to call her if we needed her but she didn't think we would. I let her father know she was holding her own and ventured downstairs to shower.

When I went back up, Britney had spiked a very high fever. We had been here before and I started doing all I had done in the past. Cold rags on her groin, neck, wrists, ankles, thighs and chest. Then I gave her the acetaminophen suppository provided by the hospice care and, though her fever didn't come down, she seemed to relax. I went from waiting mode to fix-it mode in a matter of seconds. I had fought this fever thing many times and it was something I knew how to do and, finally, I could help her. I could get her through this; I was sure of it. Plus, I was watching for all of the signs and she had none.

She looked beautiful, healthy, even radiant. She was hot to the touch and breathing more rapidly than normal but that's what happens when a person gets a high fever. After about an hour of no improvement, I sent Dr. Q a video of her breathing and asked what I should do. She replied, "Nothing". That's when it hit. But surely not. Nothing we had expected was happening. Nothing. There was no struggle, no shallow breathing and nothing else on that list we had been told to keep close by. She did seem to be intent on something but after I went down to use the restroom and came back up, she was calmer. I could see Carla talking to her over the monitor while I was downstairs and later found out that she had leaned in and told Brit she would take care of her momma. That she would take me home with her and make sure I was okay. After that, Britney was more relaxed and, though the fever wasn't coming down, her breathing had returned to normal.

Still, something wasn't right and her breathing suddenly became rapid so, at 8:15 p.m., I called the hospice nurse. She wasn't our usual nurse and needed to ask several questions so I handed the phone to Carla so that I could focus on Brit. I held her hand and rubbed her face and I told her how much we loved her and that we would all be okay. Carla, still holding the phone, leaned forward and told her to remember she was going to take care of me. At 8:20, I heard her tell the nurse she thought Brit was gone.

My world stopped. I remember feeling like I couldn't hear, everything was muffled, but I knew I had to do what I had to do. I listened to her chest, I put my nose right under her nose, I massaged her sternum and then I reached for the stethoscope. I listened for a full two minutes before I told Carla to tell the nurse that time of death was 8:23 p.m.

I wish I had never picked up that stethoscope and I haven't touched one since. For years I had listened to Brit's lungs listening for the crackle that unwanted fluid makes. I had listened for her pulse, when taking her blood pressure, and I had listened to that beautiful heart beat for twenty years. I had listened to her belly, hoping for bowel sounds, and been ecstatic when I heard some. That night, there was only silence and that silence seemed louder than any accidental thump I had heard on the end of that stethoscope in the past. That silence haunts me when the house is quiet at night or when I go under water and everything is still and silent. I called Dr. Q first and then I called my dad, who called Brit's dad for me. Then, I called Zachary. I only made three more calls. One to Jan, one to Ms. C and one to Mrs. Brady. Steph and Carla covered the rest of the list.

I don't remember much after that. I do remember lying in bed with Brit for a good hour, with my nose buried in her neck, drawing in as much of her smell as I could. I remember Steph bringing up warm water and me bathing her, cleaning out her mouth and taking that plastic button out of her belly for the first time in eleven years. I know I dressed her in warm clothes, straightened her hair and taped her blankie and part of Red's mane into her hand. Then, I covered her and sat as close beside her as I could.

I didn't cry, I didn't talk and I'm not sure I breathed. I was aware that Steph was close by and Carla had moved up behind me so I could lean on her. I remember shaking and Carla asking Steph to get Brit's robe to cover me and then just sitting there in disbelief. It didn't seem real and, though by then the nurse had arrived and checked her, what if I was wrong? What if her heart hadn't quit beating? What if she knew we thought she was gone and we were sitting there waiting for the funeral home to come and she couldn't tell me? Everything was spinning around me but I couldn't react and then, I heard the funeral home van pull up.

That's when every sense came alive and I wanted to scream and throw a fit that would have made any that Brit had thrown look like a mild tantrum. They were coming to take my baby and not to school, not on a field trip, not to a friend's house but to a refrigerator in a funeral home. It truly felt like my brain was swirling, my guts were twisting and my heart, well, it was being shattered into a million pieces that I would never put back together. I knew, in that moment, that I had a choice. I could either lose it and go completely insane or, I could do what I had prompted and soothed Brit into doing over the years. I could pull it together and deal with what I needed to deal with whether it killed me or not.

How I even thought this through in the few seconds I did is beyond me, but I chose to do what Brit had always done and held it together. I remember crying as the funeral directors came up and I remember how kind they were. They carried her down the stairs to the gurney and when they placed her on it, they told me to take all of the time I needed. I wrapped her up, all safe and warm with her stuffed pig tucked in tight, and then I kissed her and told her how much I loved her. Steph, Carla and I stood there for a minute. I kissed her one last time and covered her face and they took her to the van. It took everything in me to not scream and run after that van. I truly believe that the only thing that kept me from it, was knowing that Carla had me around the waist and I would have hurt her if I'd tried to pull away.

Then, my world went dark and blank. I've been told that Carla put me on her golf cart and brought me home, here, to her house where I have been ever since. I've been told that after I went to sleep and she went to her own bed, I wrote on Brit's page, The Blessing of Britney, and I know that's true because I've since read what I wrote. I know that Carla and I got up and went to the funeral home the next morning, where the firemen from Brit's father's fire station were standing watch over my girl. I've even been told that I spoke to them and that I made all of the plans and signed the papers. I don't remember and part of me hopes I never do.

I do remember where we went next and I remember how I defiantly said I wasn't going to cry but, the minute Ms. C opened her front door and hugged me, I dissolved. Mrs. Brady was there and we all pretended to eat lunch and I think we must have come home after that.

Chapter 20

I don't remember much of the next two weeks except trying to get the funeral all planned, meeting with different ones and staying with close friend's while Carla went out of town on a long planned trip with her friends. A trip that was much needed and, even more, deserved.

That week I stayed with close family friends, Connie and Gilbert, whose home Puppy had been staying at for the last few weeks. He was obviously confused when I came through the door by myself but he took up his post next to me instead of Brit. His unease became more and more apparent and I realized that he would never be comfortable again without using his innate ability to be a medical alert service dog.

When we had to send him away from Brit, Carla told me of a friend who had started having seizures. We reached out to him and he was eager to meet Puppy to see if they would make a good team. A few days after I came to stay at Connie's, she and I decided to take Puppy over to his home and do a trial run to see how he would do. I was a little concerned because Puppy had always had a hard time warming up to men. That day, he ran right up to his new owner and never left his side. He's been living a happy and fulfilled life with his new family and their two precious boys ever since. I will always be grateful that their bond was so immediate as I couldn't give Puppy the purpose that he needed, being a service dog. I think Brit would be very happy about Puppy's new purpose.

From the day Britney died to the day of her funeral was exactly two weeks. Most of the time, I stayed busy running errands and getting everything in order, much like I would imagine a mother would do as she prepared for her daughter's wedding. I knew that this celebration of life was the very last wish I could carry out for Britney. Making sure it was done exactly as she had written, gave me something to focus on and helped me function.

Other times, I was a mess. Had Connie not known me all my life, she would have not known how to help me through. Even then, she was dealing with a me that none of us had ever seen before. In the past, I had been incredibly strong, even stoic, no matter what life had thrown at me. From the time I was a child, through rocky teenage years and through twenty years of one medical emergency after another, nothing fazed me. Nothing made me lose control and nothing got the best of me because I had mastered the use of mind over matter. I couldn't afford to lose control and I certainly couldn't take a chance of needing anyone to lean on because frankly, I didn't have anyone. Yes, I had support but my support was coming from those who had their own families to raise and their own lives to live. I'm so grateful for the time they took away from their own families to step in and support us in any way they could. While I know Brit and I couldn't have made it as long as we did without their support, I do feel that not having consistent support at home benefitted me in staying strong. I know that being strong, and on my own, allowed me to do what I needed to do for Britney. However, not knowing how or when to lean on others has become the biggest obstacle in my healing.

Connie and Gilbert did all they could to show me that no matter what emotional state I was in, they were there to support me. They weren't the only ones seeing a whole new side of me. I was completely blindsided by my emotions and my inability to rein them in. For the first time in my life, I truly had no control. I was feeling emotions I had stuffed for years, and with the lack of control and added feelings, came a fear that I can't describe. The sadness was desperate. It felt like I needed to cry, choke, yawn and take a deep breath all at once. Only I couldn't. I couldn't even do one of these things, yet I would find myself holding my breath without even realizing it. All I could do was lie on the bed, hold Brit's robe and let whatever wave rolled over me have its way and then, after it subsided, I'd get up and keep going.

Because I was determined to carry out the wishes Brit had taken the time to write out, I kept going. I ordered pictures and shopped for frames to put them in. I met with ministers and downloaded music to be delivered to the church. I delivered pictures for her slideshow to my cousin, who did an amazing job of bringing them to life and setting them to music. Still, it seemed so unjust for a short slideshow to exemplify all of the wonderful, brilliant and beautiful moments and accomplishments that made up her life. We didn't have enough hours or days to make a slideshow long enough to truly portray the life of our Aggie, our animal lover, our horsewoman, our brilliant scientist and all of the other things that she was. We didn't have enough time to make any slideshow that would show the depth and the richness that was her life, my baby's life. A life full of so much good but not enough good to counter the suffering her body had thrown at her every step of the way. I still can't watch that slideshow without the unfairness of it all consuming me.

I want to be angry. When I see my beautiful, brown-eyed, curly-haired girl smiling in that slideshow, it's hard for me to remember that she is truly in a better place now. I didn't take a lot of pictures of her in the hospital, when she was in pain or the general sad pictures that would help me remember how she struggled. While I'm glad I don't have those types of pictures, I feel like they would help me focus more on the healing she is experiencing now. When I'm hurting and all I can envision is the happy moments, the unjustness of it all hits the hardest. Still, I can't get angry and as much as I'd like to blame someone, I can't blame God.

I wish I could. I'll admit that. I truly wish I could blame and get angry with God. If I only remember the happy times, I almost can make myself go there but even then, reality creeps in. I may not have a lot of pictures to remind me of her suffering or of the times in the hospitals, but I have all the memories in my head. Only the fact that I know where she is, and that she is healthy and whole, gets me through. I can't get angry at God. I can only thank Him.

Chapter 21

Even under the most normal of circumstances, no one likes to go to a funeral. We all do it because it's the right thing to do, for the ones left behind, but none of us find joy in a funeral. Under normal circumstances, the person whose life you are there to celebrate is typically older and has had many years to experience their life. While this doesn't take away the pain, it is the natural order of things, and we all go pay our respects and listen to stories of a life well lived. When you're attending the funeral of a child or a young person, there's nothing natural about it. No one wants to be there because, not only is it hard to imagine how something like this could have happened, it's hard to watch the parents and the siblings. While we all want to show our support, none of us know what to say and none of us want to imagine ourselves in their place. I'd like to think that Brit's funeral was filled with good memories and some measure of comfort for her peers, but I still know that it was very hard for everyone.

I will be forever grateful for the hundreds of people who attended in person and the thousands who watched online. I remember sitting there long after the service started and seeing the line to sign her memory book still stretched well past the doors. I know that the crowd was there to support us but I also know that, had it not been for Britney's life and legacy, most of those people wouldn't even know who we were.

As I sat there just as Brit had written, with Ms. C beside me and no flowers on the stage, all I could think of was how honored she must be as she looked down at us from heaven. I'm sure she giggled as Mr. Jay read the stories that her teachers contributed. I'm sure she was proud as her brother stood on the stage and sang a song just for her. I know she was happy as Tanner prayed not only for her, but for her beloved Puppy. I'd like to hope that she was proud of how I worked to put it all together just as she had planned. I know, without a doubt, that the part she would have loved most was when Mr. Willson stood, softly called the Muster and the Aggie War Hymn played boldly for the recessional as her funeral came to an end. Hundreds of people came forward to offer condolences and share their stories of how Brit had touched their lives. It seemed like hours before the crowd dwindled down and I appreciated every single person who came up to speak to me.

I had held it together for two weeks, and as soon as we got in the car I fell asleep in the back seat. I knew nothing until we were home and parked in the garage. The minute I walked into my room, it all hit. For twenty years I had had the most honorable, fulfilling job God could have ever entrusted me with and, though I'm still a mother to Zachary, I was suddenly retired. As I walked into that room I realized that I no longer had a purpose, my days would never be the same, my thoughts wouldn't constantly be consumed with Brit's care and I no longer knew who I was. That was when I gave up, lay on my bed and gave in to the tears but only for a little while. Dr. Q and Carla didn't let me give in for too long.

Typically, the funeral holds some finality for most people. The grief doesn't end but everyone has paid their respects, and life tends to settle back down and go on. Not for Britney. She had left such a legacy that almost daily I would receive cards and packages in the mail, emails from professors and all types of plaques and memorabilia from Texas A&M. There were also weekly calls from doctors, nurses, teachers and so many whose lives Britney had touched while they touched hers. Those calls are still coming more than a year after she left us. All of these sentiments have come at just the right times and all of them have meant so much.

When I was contacted by the Texas A&M Traditions Council, I should not have been surprised by the emotions that hit me. I was happy that they wanted to honor her yet sad that they had reason to. I was touched by the amount of students who had noticed she wasn't on campus, and searched to find out why, but so badly wished she was still sitting in class with them. Most of all, I was beyond proud of her and so very honored that her fellow students wanted to remember her during their next Silver Taps Memorial Ceremony. Had I known when they contacted me, exactly what this memorial entailed, I would have been even more touched.

Sometime in the weeks leading up to Silver Taps, Carla and I spent the weekend cleaning out my and Brit's apartment in College Station. Silver Taps is the first Tuesday of each month so we decided we would go early that day and finish cleaning the apartment before heading to campus and attending the ceremony. It was hot and I'd had more than my share of crying spells when we finally got settled in the Aggie Hotel. We had all decided to take naps, but I couldn't relax, and decided to go walk the campus that Brit and I had walked so many times before.

When we left home, to head to College Station, for some reason I decided to go back in and take a small vial of Brit's ashes with us. I had no plans and had never felt compelled to take her with me anywhere before. I wanted to take her with me when I went back to Aggieland this one last time. As I walked out the door to walk the campus, I made sure I carried her with me. Our good friend, Cindy, had traveled with us and she decided to walk with me. I had no real plans. I just wanted to walk where we had walked and hope that somehow Brit would join me and I could feel her with me one more time. We walked past all of the memorial markers that students had stopped to pay their respects at since dawn that morning. There were flowers, mementos and thousands of cards left by fellow students and the more I read, the more I just knew that this campus was truly Brit's home. That's when I realized why I had felt the need to carry part of her with me and I went in search of that age-old landmark, the place where so many memories are made for Aggies. I knew Brit was guiding me and I knew that I was going to leave a part of her where I knew she would want to be.

As I walked up to the Century Tree, the sun was shining on it and there were no students around. At the time, I didn't know if it was legal or not, but every part of me knew what I had to do. Cindy said a prayer and then stepped aside as I crawled under that Century Tree and spread part of Britney on every root I could find. I didn't cry and I didn't even feel sad because I knew that this would have made her so incredibly happy. As it softly rained the next morning, I imagined how she would be a part of that tree and this hallowed ground forever more.

That evening we were led to the family reception area where we waited for the ceremony to start. As we were led from that area to our seats on the Academic Plaza, "How Great Thou Art" and "Amazing

Grace" played from the Albritton Bell Tower. It was dead silent and pitch dark because all of the lights on campus had been extinguished and each student had silenced their devices, and their voices, in honor of their fallen comrades. I could make out a few shadows and could tell there were hundreds of students standing watch. I later found out there were over thirteen thousand attending Silver Taps that night. At 10:30 p.m., the Ross Volunteer Company marched silently into the Academic Plaza where they fired a three-volley salute in honor of their fallen Aggies. As the last volley was fired, buglers atop the Academic Building began to play their version of "Taps". A version unique only to Texas A&M and better known as "Silver Taps". The buglers played "Taps" once to the north, once to the south then, to the west but never the east. The sun has set and will never rise on that fallen Aggie ever again.

I will never come up with the words to describe the honor that I, and everyone attending that ceremony with me, felt. Thousands had come out late that night, stood there in silence and knew that we had no way of seeing them or knowing they were there. They came to honor Britney and I have no doubt that she knew that each and every one of them was there.

As we pulled out the next morning, I fought a battle with my emotions most of the way home. I had left a little part of Britney and a large part of myself on that campus and I knew it was highly unlikely I'd ever return again. We drove home the same route Brit and I had driven countless times before and passed all of the typical places we had stopped along the way. Through all of my time of grief, that trip home was the longest amount of time that grief came to visit but sat down and stayed.

Again, it seemed like this would have been a finality but Brit is an Aggie and Aggies are never forgotten. In April, we attended Muster, the Roll Call for the Absent. I chose to attend the one in Fort Worth because it was closer to home. So that evening, in College Station, as Britney's name was read, one of her close friends was standing in Reed Arena holding a candle in her honor. At the ceremony I attended, Dr. T, her doctor of twelve years and her fellow Aggie, held the candle in her honor.

As hundreds of names of fallen Aggies were read, we each responded,

"Here" to acknowledge that Aggie present in spirit. The list went on and on and, with each name, we were getting closer to Britney's. As honored as I was to be a part of this ceremony, I didn't want to hear her name called. However, there was a small sense of comfort knowing that she would be okay with it because, after all, it was an Aggie tradition and she was an Aggie through and through. As an Aggie mom, I was proud to know that she was part of a family of such great traditions but that didn't keep my heart from pounding as we got closer to her name. Everyone in the room was standing out of respect and I felt my legs getting weak. I held my breath, tried to keep myself from shaking so badly and prayed I wouldn't hear her name. No amount of wishing or trying to pray it all away could stop what I knew I was about to hear.

So, it was read "Ms. Britney Gavitt", and her comrades answered, "Here".

Words from Carla, Steph and Dr Q:

"I don't know what the main reason was that made me love Britney. Besides the fact that she was ethereally beautiful, and brilliant, she was so innocent and timid looking. Of course, her being sick makes you want to take care of her, even though she was much taller than me and could take care of herself, thank you. Just being with her made me want to learn everything about everything. A few words from me would either cause her to agree or cause a well intentioned "Well, actually" to be said before I got schooled on the subject that apparently I knew nothing about. I loved it! She was so good at jigsaw puzzles and I would watch her putting in ten pieces to my one. I kept a puzzle out for her and me to work. I told her not to worry about her mother because I would be here for her. I gave my word to Brit that I would help Holly, no matter what happened and she said thank you. I will miss Britney and her critique of my driving forever even though my driving is not bad, just fast. Not knowing her for very long really didn't matter, she was loved quickly and deeply. Thank you for riding my carousel roller coaster Brit! And thank you for giving me the honor of being one of *your* people. I love you Brit!"

—Carla

"Oh Brit, where do I even begin? In the eleven or twelve short years I knew you, we sparked a special friendship full of silliness, laughter, smart remarks and lots of eye rolling on your part. Apart from helping your mom give you care, I would do anything to distract you from some of the constant pain you were in. There was no amount of embarrassing lengths I wouldn't go to just to make you laugh. Your vocabulary and intellect was so far beyond your years and beyond most people. You were my absolute hero!

Of course you were at the top of your class in school and later in college. Boy was Texas A&M lucky to win your allegiance from those northern Ivy League schools. I knew your beautiful mind and intellect would challenge and amaze the world. Your genius, your amazing horsemanship and your mind-blowing ability to communicate with all animals were truly gifts from God. You were a gift from God, to everyone that had the honor to meet you.

I watched your mom suffer as she watched your decline, and it was heart wrenching. I watched as she went without sleep for weeks on end while taking care of you. If I were to be in her shoes, I would hope to be as brave as she was, in letting my child decide when it was time to stop fighting.

Brit, I dream of you and you are healthy, happy and smiling down at us. I wish I could have been present when you asked God all the questions that you had planned. I can't wait to see you again and I know you will come riding up on Red to greet me, in that great ranch in the sky. I love you Brit!

—Steph.

Britney was a young girl who had to grow up too fast due to her circumstances. She was a challenge from in utero, but we knew she was worth holding on to. Who knew those lungs, heard all over the OB floor, were destined to be heard by more than just close family? And, she was so cute, so who cared? Over the years, she met every challenge with the stoicism of a well-weathered pinwheel that has stood the test of time. She had a life dream of going to A&M and she was determined to get there. And, by golly she did! She was smart as a whip but well mannered enough to tolerate those less inclined. I was honored to be considered somewhere above the base, but always thought she knew more than I did. She could always make me smile, like when she decided to wear the Mardi gras beads I brought back, all at one time, or sleep with the giant Cat in the Hat. She was brave, smart, kind and quiet yet reserved at the same time. She always kept you guessing. I have been honored to be a part of her life and look forward to seeing her in the next one.

—Dr. Q

Epilogue

So, here we all are…without the physical presence of Britney, but she's always with us. Even when the weather is too cold for butterflies, we see them all around us. Usually it's one very persistent, very pretty, very forthright and noticeable butterfly that comes daily and actually follows us around. She lands on one of us often and no amount of poking at her will make her fly away. It's very odd the way the butterfly seems to demand to be noticed. It is not always the same butterfly but the manner in which she acts is always the same. Of course, we know Britney is not a butterfly, but we're always looking for confirmation that our loved ones are still with us, one way or another.

The four of us who spent Britney's last weeks with her are trying our best to carry on. To try to live for the moments she was robbed of and try to make her proud as she looks down on us. Those last weeks will always be etched in our memories, and no matter how hard we try, we will never outlive them.

Those were despondent times, horrific times and cruel times. We three were despondent because we watched this brave, young girl make a decision that most adults will never have to make. It was horrible to realize that her body had let her down, but it had; it was worn out. We watched her make the hard decisions on how she was going to win her battle and let her unrelenting pain come to an end. Not one of us could accompany her past that end and she knew it. She also knew that if she had to face death, she was going to do it on her terms and no one else's.

Most of all, those times were trumped by Britney's bravery, grace and grit. We are so proud that Britney allowed us to be her honor guard and stand at her side as she truly and surely gained her wings. It was a blessing to witness as she entered into the realm of heaven and the presence of God.

It was especially cruel for me, as I had fought for her and protected her to the best of my ability her entire life. I was left behind to mourn and suffer her loss and her loss feels like a failure on my part. Most times, I feel like I'm stuck on September 4, 2021. I've been told I've made progress in my grief but it doesn't feel like it. I try to make every day one that Britney would be proud of but I'm thinking she would be rolling her eyes at me most of the time. I feel like I'm wallowing in grief sometimes and I know she would not approve. I am trying to start a new life, but life right now, seems to have no purpose. My children have been my purpose for twenty-five years. Now, Zach is grown and making a life for himself and Brit, she's gone and living a life we can only imagine. Still, purpose or not, I am determined to survive and to cope with everything that has happened. I will keep Britney's legacy alive and eventually help others deal with their own grief.

I am blessed, beyond blessed. I am still here, still at the same house and still sleeping in the same bed I was brought home to after Britney passed from this life. Had I not been brought here, to Bill and Carla's, I wouldn't have healed the little bit I have. I know without a doubt that, though it was Brit's plan, it was ultimately a gift from God. A gift at the very worst time of my life. A gift that has taught me to slow down, live in the moment, accept love, rest in security and not be so hard on myself. I've learned to take one day, one hour, one minute and even just one step at a time.

One step, that's all it takes, to move forward, and I will. I will keep going, keep taking steps and keep moving forward, all the while remembering who taught me to do just that.

Love you Baby Girl, with all of my heart. Momma's proud of you!

About the Authors

Holly devoted twenty years of her life to walking beside her daughter, Britney, keeping her alive while she pursued her dreams. Britney passed away in September 2021. This is Holly's first book.

Carla came to know Britney in the last year of her life but became a trusted friend and one of Britney's biggest comforts. Carla made a promise to Britney to take care of her momma and it was with Carla's prompting that this book was finished and completed in honor of Britney.

Printed in the United States
by Baker & Taylor Publisher Services